In memory of my Uncle

Ken

There once was a young man named ken,
who found in a drawer an old pen,
And as you might think,
He filled it with ink,
And wrote a new poem in his den.

*Jim*

Thomas James Lawton
Uncle Navy Aviator Veteran Author
1928-2016
Buried at sea

# In the Moment

## Ken Krizan

authorHOUSE®

AuthorHouse™
1663 Liberty Drive
Bloomington, IN 47403
www.authorhouse.com
Phone: 1 (800) 839-8640

Published by AuthorHouse   09/13/2016

ISBN: 978-1-5246-0211-6 (sc)
ISBN: 978-1-5246-0212-3 (hc)
ISBN: 978-1-5246-0210-9 (e)

Print information available on the last page.

Any people depicted in stock imagery provided by Thinkstock are models,
and such images are being used for illustrative purposes only.
Certain stock imagery © Thinkstock.

This book is printed on acid-free paper.

# Contents

# Preface

The words that follow rhyme rhythm reason are notes in the Symphony of my life. Write what is out of heart in the moment. Surmised unasked questions are unanswered and leave thoughts imprisoned. Searched the blend between fact fiction fantasy some call written history for the ages. Realized the theme of these pages is existential. There is no world if you do not embrace it. How can one swim without water breath without air think without consciousness?

# Acknowledgements

Want to thank all of the prodding, encouragement insight
from my children John & Karen, grandchildren Sam,
Magge & Kristyn and especially my uncle Jim.

This is a legacy of my emigrant great great grandfather,
Julius Simon Krzyczanowski, (adopted), Danzig, West Prussia.
A Prussian Army Officer forced to leave with his family
to the United States because he was Catholic.
Also my great grandfather Carl Oscar Colbornson, smithy
horse whisperer, Allamakee County and my grandfather
Eugene Irving Lawton, owner, editor, publisher of a weekly
news paper 'The Victor Record', Iowa

# Chapter I
## Dawn of Time

*Life can only be understood backwards,
But it must be lived forwards.
-- Soren Kierkegaard*

# The Alone Man

Since that instant of birth out of the womb unattached
Breathing earth air the first time happily crying I am alive
Roll over crawl on hands and knees moving up stand walk
In your habited space occupied one step at a time aftertime
Going forward backward dancing tripping running the race
Pause and realize consciousness of self being

Think only what one mind has in thought awake sleeping
Learn at own unique rate of retention loss in between
Existential individual story of a single life on skewed lines
Private travels in air on land out to sea blindly with insight
Personal journey from humble beginning illusion in progress
Face in the mirror reflection you one to see blink wink nod

Has tear of happiness laughter resounding around in air
Heart elevated into weightlessness parachute floating
Tis with great sorrow the destiny of life is for all over
Known spirit is the last spark one has to the end
Some ebb and tide others fly on a breeze
We all are a breath away from unconsciousness

Silent path forest green fern mossy carpet canopy turquoise sky
Cardinal across rill echoing into the breeze a song to another
Ushering in a faint sound of waterfall trickle over the hill
Moving among the sun made shadows bright to dark
Bringing to sight visual images of ink blots waving
Alive living tree canopy of leaves overhead under foot

Animated beings surrounding encompassing embracing man
Sensing primordial presence as an unseen motion aura karma
By my side with each stride the memories flashing light bulbs
Say please stay and be one of us all forever never was to be
A bond forged before dawn of time...life is death-death life
Alone man lives life inside their alpha and omega

# Vanished Cemetery Revisited

Alone man walks touches talks among the future dead
Going to destinations one foot confronting ground at a time
Pulling perpendicularly transverse to gravity of earths mass
Anticipating next step unconsciously learned from youth
Breathing in out along path ways of your living journey

Open eyes watching the canvas of continuous vision unravel
Scroll colored carpetry like a TV image with great detail
Do we live behind the masks or does the façade take over
So we fake who we are on purpose to others with false feelings
Unrevealed by talk inflection action reaction demeanor face

Realize hide to conceal sins of the heart gone unnoticed
Form of menagerie caricature on merry-go-round ride
Deep inside buried from light just a complex soul vagabond
Methinks walking thru head stones where have they all gone
None came back cept in deep sleep dreams awake thoughts

Understand destiny will join others when it is time
Must make each moment something to enjoy as much as can
Blood from vena cava into auricle ventricle lung back to heart
Beat unending until the last contraction pulse systolic
Timing is most everything and I am only now

Alone man lives from beginning with only self
Life is totality of human lived experiences
Found key to happiness during living existence
Came to know compassion for others is virtuous
Being kind to less fortunate a gift of heart

*The strongest man in the world is*
*he who stands most alone.*
*Henrik Ibsen*

# Unflinchingly

Scythe handle raps at the door
Not time for crescendo or go Erato
Flamenco enjoyed with tequila
Ballet wine aurora australis awe

The way we were is not now
Experience moment to moment passing
Continuous river ever flowing
Desert ocean rippling waves of sand

Everyone is left behind at a point
The rest evolve in to future
Nothing written true before happening
Omen in minds of superstitious

There is no constancy to apparition
Some want to rule the world
Bottom feeder end up where they are
Not all change one way or another

People born with tiger stripes
Bigger smaller bigoted compassionate
Listen to inner voice width breath
Follow that which you feel in heart

Existence on earth irrelevant
Survival to the last all that's left
Wan-a-do reject eject cerebral flight
Hoped to stop ship would not

Happy days are that for just one or many
Children do not know what reality is
Into the valley shadow not to reason why
'Great Expectation' poor orphan stays alive

To remember forget not a choice gone
It was once a cabaret youth
Cant make one want others
Lance in heart leaves scars inside out

Long ago tune evokes passion memories
Orange ember branded deep into core
Transcendental aura pervade ethereal essence
Fetal heart beat evidence of life presence

# Façade Melting

Ocean of life just sail away to destiny
Serendipitous tsunami doldrums abyss
Castaway to unknown shoals off dunes
Staying aware so easy when young spry
Only alive because blood keeps pumping

Soar above clouds as eagle feel elation joy of...
Thoughts racing across skyscape after the...
Never to know the mysteries of being to...
Standing to feel the cosmos still yet...
The rest of your life is ahead of...

Isobars coming closer to each other wind
A vacant space in milieu for another gale
Single drone of many vying for one queen
Let the children dance into their future
Every where once roamed a first step

It was brief moment in eternity
Evening tarry till morn yet dreamily
Pain of mind experience not felt by tissue
Lightness of dark not seen by blind voyeur
Sound to deaf vibration sense in space

Living is made ideas rhyme farewell
Time just standing watching as go on
Been that way all of past slipping gone done
Never retrievable once twice ebbing in memory
Iconoclastic when end reached personal erased

Others change self changes with the breeze
Left lost just still in universe deep freeze
Be what who am every second
What reason for us to persist exist
Think walk alone as one

# Desperate Enigma

Progression of thought ebb flow thru time
Not evolution too short though may be sublime
Eventual supremacy of reason a myth
Wrinkled face appears map to monolith
See what you want to see
Sea to shinning sea

Cloaked enigma magma desperate to last
Bubonic hysteria devastation victim of past
Fantasy reality not choice which best
There no key to open treasure chest
Some things are never forgot
Especially those who be bigot

Some don't always reap what sown
Till plant seed leave rain life grown
Don't matter what learnt think ignore
All is what you feel nothing less more
Piece of the rainbow illusionarily dealt
Eventually will be reconstituted regardless felt

Been kicked around up down routine
Felt but blocked out what ever pain
Learn cower submit to lash on bare flesh
Slave never gone from thought only hope wish
Turn round move on dig inside searching
Four winds hit minds eye with fist reaching

True control not power without compassion
Languor touch not wanted is self depression
We born innocent taught learn love hate
Sanctuary cell block battle ground one fate
Under currents rip tides waves feelings adrift
Mind moves without wind sail caught in rift

Most things get wet in the horizontal rain
Duel steel rails under a travelling train
Zebras cant change their spots leopard stripes
Neither may man escape essence with gripes
Eagles some times walk while lynx soars
Irony is perception that has many oars

Awakened by massive din of silence
One could surmise from mere existence
It is not the years in one life
Rather the life in years of strife
Last moment touched most previous
Remembered thought of one consciousness

# Alive!

got to the end of the road
life continued on
blown leaves rolling over others
crabs ebbing to wave edge on sandy beach
continuous basaltic igneous land genesis

unending ending infinity

place we live in is within
an impenetrable space of sacred self
all knowledge will some day lost
purest sense heart flees to be free

conclusion unknown gone

traverse the unending high way
as essence pulsates
eagle soars against thousand foot cliff
midst thermo
minds path has only one way to go
next second op
thoughts crops populations to feed

situations dictations choices

at end of road trail descends toward abyss
and yet life force lingers with hope
deep psyche promotes optimism a smile
be reborn to fate accept live with it

visit to the Animal Fair

# Naked Pen

Time without worth is waste
a Pterodactyl flight
Gone never to return into
deeper than eye heart insight

Want is not have
life what be your reality
Love is only forever soul eclipse
belongs to totality

Glowing in memory dreams
lost past part of one self
All knowledge within attempt
to pass on collecting dust on shelf

*Adversity is the first path to truth.*
*— Lord George Byron*

# Chapter II
## Lifescape Existence

*Nothing in this world is so powerful as an idea whose time has come.*
*Victor Hugo*

# Cala Deya Cliff Dive

Stars stationary planets arranged special order space
The mystic metaphysical magnet pulling me to a place
Was meant to fly over ocean mountains then to realize
An epiphany to nurture on a majestic island paradise
Basked under Mediterranean Sea sun in summertime
Combed sand beaches dipped body in the water brine

Traversed winding roadway overland to opposite side of isle
Destination Cala Deya sides towering buttes length one mile
A small beach village Cantina shacks no tourists warm sand
North cliff jutting up straight pinnacle platform highest land
Arduous life's experiences prepares oneself to quest attain awe
A singular artistic movement to be seen but few never by all

Fishing boats enter cove stop indigenous jump frolic in sea
Moment effused up from the gut I dare myself a god to be
Walked to the lapping waves waded dove swam to rocky base
Found smooth weathered boulders looked upward did face
Preceded through the hard low sage brush apex was to seek
Sometimes craggy steepness on all fours zigzag to reach peak

I moved to the edge looked around out to the West horizon
Who might have been at this spot millennium past denizen
Only who know what this height was when preparing plunge
Would fathom the nerve to place life at extreme peril a lunge
Time went by flashing back to thousands of flights into space
Curled toes tight over ell edge slowly position physique in place

Embody Zeus edifice statuesque atop Olympus sierra
Sun light streaks thru hazy aura enshrouding vista
Against azure cloudless sky appears a mythical deific
Real surrealistic effervescent preeminence of an epic
Perception slips into a natural meditative existence
Heart beat breath changes into slow motion presence

Pushed off soaring into a flying swan the air rushing by
Pointing toes and arching spine slow move to a vertical lie
Brought two fists beneath just before placid liquid surface
Into Poseidon depths up with champagne bubbles to efface
Burst the water gasping waved hand to shore all was right
An inane feat brief insanity will be in memory my last night

# Spaceship Journey

Sounds float on the warm light summer breeze calling
People walking by with children chairs blankets talking
Park band stage beckons keep on coming my darling to me
Minds waiting free performing arts concert in camaraderie
As bodies arrive bringing heart and soul in logic proportion
Feelings swell from number to number each elicited reflection

Inspiration is in the score notes lyrics seen on the singer's lips
Before man was man phonetic communication was voice quips
If only you believed what I believe we would just sail away
Performers pushing lung air through larynx put on display
Infection rhythms vibrating resonating of the guitar strings
Being alone together witnessing event a joy at this time brings

Amazing noise of a choreographic symphony evoking emotion
The synaptic catharses of pleasing healing more than notion
An electric solo both hands in synchronicity so empowering
Starting as if leaping into air building crescendo towering
To be one's own turning slide sway dance testing the limits
What one has now is within us coming out precious minutes

Faint smell of recent mown grass where the crowd has come to sit
Standing moving around with dogs coolers all in a big jigsaw fit
A wooden ship on the water clapping shouting like rolling waves
Clear sociological phenomenon picturing how there masses behaves
It is not what you wanted it is what needed you came to bear
Here for your self pleasing to show the band how much you care

First crescent moon moving across a light then into dark sky
Why the rainbow human cross section came but to get high and fly
Exhilaration ambience injects endorphins into the machine
Fueling a full energy experience some portions a surrealistic dream
Sticks of the drum beat its cadence to many renditions of art
Instruments add gives a signature and then voice of the heart

Cool night air comes in replacing the heat from the day's bright sun
It was never hot nor cold just perfect
temperature no stress more fun
Becoming evident it is winding down all liquid libations near gone
Appreciation expressed heavily now following each song set a tone
The final ending has come band lines up on stage holds hands bows
Evening with The Jefferson Starship you could almost hear the wows

# Fickled Burlesque

Train of thought is not guided by two rail tracks to carnage
Mind travels the intelligent imagination whims of knowledge
Soars into the blue white sky clouds searching for inspiration
Plunging to bottom of the sea to think in deep concentration
Swim thru wet hot magma and reach the core to understand
Enter the vacuum of space in a hope to further life's demand

Change your mind adjust sails go in a different direction
Go where you want down wind into it tacking adaptation
Again aim for the ideal yet anticipate pit falls along the way
Sometimes when it seems all is lost you end up a win so to say
And turn round another moment has been won no all is lost
There are no greats in wealth poverty fame there always is cost

Lift mine eyes to the real make up mascara just a clown deal
Genuine article does not have to advertise just have a fine feel
One person smashes into your presence it is not a set constancy
Body moving with a grace innocence inner beauty past fantasy
Sight riveted to the infrastructure of your mind unleashingly
Face in the mirror of tranquility not to ever leave unabashedly

Those fascinations obsessions spreading over tingling bare skin
Not thinking about nothing else she is a prize could never win
Taken every day by the masses never a chance to even speak to
Her mind is a career degree not to acknowledge has no clue
Impossible to have a semblance of ever being with her never
Cold reality freezing the resulting in big case of love fever

Smitten by the pseudo opportunity a guile with no shelf life
Must stop the unwarranted obsession and cut it off with a knife
Self torture masochism of masculinity fading with time
Unable to blind the eyes of my mask in my id to ego crime
All thoughts originate in the cranium to burst out when
Moments thinking try to cast out but impossible the yen

They say for me to move on move on them could never be me
Die is cast live in the self cage no lock no escape not likely
Can not stop on the path turn around go back to square one
Does not work that way in reality some races can never be won
Give up those alternatives though worse just take the hemlock
Fate hands our liver on a block and future to the last tick tock

*What is done from love is always beyond good and evil.*
*Friedrich Nietzsche*

# I Am a River

I am a river wet moving from an up stream source
Rolling down hill taking the least resistant course
Meandering curling one way then a different direction
Pushing against the shore cutting into rock soil erosion
Fed by mother natures milk from heavens high cloud
Hail snow sleet shower rain accompanying thunder loud

As the sky stays dry moisture dwindles as flow to where bound
After a time river evolves into the deep hidden underground
Moving down seeping thru cracks openings along geosynclines
Some arroyo beds are ancient pathways never in straight lines
Changing constantly with earth movements as they happen
Ever filtering into vast caverns cauldrons aquifers to dampen

Earthquakes up down sideways some over others under
Causing variations in stop hold up let go again further
Traveling at rates according to the rock and land geology
Moving between sand gravel dirt cracked stone topography
Gravity guiding the liquid thru the many labyrinths caves
Like many conduit channels gravities ebb and tide waves

Running across hard surface rushing toward a water fall
Cascading over the edge of the world end like a cannon ball
Splashing up in air then speeding downward into the abyss
Molecules misting a dynamic hydrology machine to witness
Some parts evaporating to make the humidity rise skyward
The earth's circular cycles of vapor constantly moving forward

Friction from the void of space against the earth's rotation
Creating the clouds architecture in forming and motion
Physics of fluid mechanics is a driving engine of weather
When conditions are ripe moisture falls in the atmosphere
The wind heat cold transformed by far away solar influence
Mist a visible refraction spectrum of rainbows arc of effervesce

Reasons whether there is too much or very little precipitation
Consistent rain along with the snow melt feeds life vegetation
Amounts are governed by many known and unknown things
Rivers flooding high over their banks a new channel it brings
This ultimately caused by the vast oceans lakes rivers evanesce
Without the water course stream life would not be in existence

# Collective Mindful Meditation

At birth there is no remembered awareness of consciousness
Initially infant's behavior is governed by sensuousness
After many years of pubescence driven by secretory glands
Production of body hormones for various biological plans
Thru the formative years the mind becomes to be aware
Sensibility a learning process to actually know how to care

Eventually a mindful engagement begins into contemplation
At a moment one realizes their own conscious imagination
A pursuit of knowledge to understand the meaning of life
Some are disillusioned by variations of unrelenting strife
Searching to find that one why question to be answered
What is our purpose and to make clear what is blurred

One needs to enter a journey into mindful meditation
Using those tools of life's experiences in reflection
Traveling in the minds pathways to focus inward
Extraction from inner feelings something to go forward
Each individual has their way of dealing with psyche
It could or not take a life time to ultimate finality

Many are like a sheep and follows the whole flock
Suppositions unstable as quicksand or strong as bed rock
There is comfort in having friends with the same ideal
Being and going along with others helps how you feel
Even though we seem to live happy we are still alone
Climb the mountains cross deserts oceans finish as one

Scheme of existential living can not be without communalism
Innately being singular we all need a coping mechanism
And must come together in a setting of peaceful existence
Establishing neutral dialogue to be in each others presence
Discuss commonalities ideologies with intelligent candor
And appreciate even though not agreeing with my savor

The world of today is shying away from We to the Me
Self has become more important than camaraderie
A compassionate group will collectively help one in need
Modern societies have evolved into the thralls of a greed
There is no escape from who we are or how we may think
Main goal should be to find commonality the missing link

# Dance in Heart

Dancing performing a gift since the dawn of time
It is like poetry put to step both reason and rhyme
First muscle contraction to last a scene of beauty
Not a second unthought there is no room for futility
A youth art demonstrated outward when prancing
Inside the performer they show by overtly advancing

Human body in a synchronicity to the music rhythm
Movement flowing like the swinging of a pendulum
Straight legged pointed toes rise up an over the head
Spinning arms move in out stop and go no notes read
Brain seizes that moment crescendoing into ecstasy
Consciously flexing operant learning with no hesitancy

Not looking back not forward it is the now performance
Learning the choreography all over the stage distance
At that wooden section no thought other than motion
Feelings real surrealistic connection of each gyration
Epiphany deep within to finally know this is my destiny
Reaching to that inner talent to move more gracefully

Twirling head around front again to face audience
A fluid dance this way that memory directed cadence
Touching the floor leaving the surface into air space
Constantly changing figurine crossing vision in grace
Never losing the unwritten score keeping in the mind set
Practice and fitness seen in the performance not past yet

Like a crystal clear stream rolling over smooth stone
From the ground up a kinesiology study of body tone
Transpiring thru creative nuance emanating from soul
A picture record for posterity etched in a photo journal
Applause appreciation sets quest to perform again some day
This moment just a prelude to a career hopefully on the way

There are steps for many reasons as we go from here to there
So many miles have been in bare feet or some shoes to ware
Drama to have the gift is so serious for less dancers than few
Grew into a pampered milieu blessed with a lessoned sinew
Praise is deserved in the ultimate time sacrifice dedication
Focused on that ever next exercise to rise into self perfection

*Don't compromise yourself. You are all you've got.*
*Janis Joplin*

# Rhythmic Passions

Went to the ballet to take a glance at real dance
From up close to a distance a symphony of prance
The dawn of mankind movement has never stood still
Synchronicity from heart made by foot what the thrill
Life's dedications lessons training wanting to perform
Natural talent core choreographic steps to proscenium

Start at four in academy so what you want to do
Other girls few boys begin to learn cadence milieu
Many friendships melding side by side know forever
Parent chauffeuring to from floor seems never over
A regimen through out the formative years so clear
If a boy goes the distance on toes becomes danseur

Pull on leotard straps over shoulders laces tie up shoes
Blank smile on face as troupe ready adorned in tutus
First occasion to dance all practiced only butterfly's fears
It all becomes worthwhile to mom dad these are dears
A step into the future lime light is who you have become
Many miles have been traveled now done glad to be home

Next show sessions away stretching exercise endurance
Strong hand soft heart instructors make true difference
Some times it feels like running a marathon race
Your compassionate mentor keeps focus on the pace
Staying on a schedule the physical mental a task
Only one to be the principle many in support cast

The day will come when dreams will come true
Costume fitted make up tiara on moment pure
Orchestra begins overture waiting side stage
Curtains open and you burst from inner cage
Your performance never to be forgotten in time
Soul so ready and has ripened into your prime

Think back look forward now is moment to choose
There is only one past in present you win or lose
Continue to better who you are for a long way to go
Mind and body matures movement as it will flow
What the next step makes influences who you are
This is your life leap into the spin round aware

# As Time Goes By

Blink elicited spark thru axonal impulses conduction
Point from to synapses electricity speed expedition
Like a life passing flashing across the brain screen
All the moments of existence brought forth to be seen
If tomorrow is to happen then it becomes our day
Time still start again every instant now not to stay

Thoughts of those full rainbows as they'd glimmer
Remembering the ground shaking earthquakes shimmer
Surrender to true love from seeing as her eyes gleam
And the split second it took for the smiles beam
Disregard what wise men say for only fools rush in
It matters that sentient consciousness is ready to begin

Each solo intellect interpreting feelings last to now
Forming wanting wishing to go forward and avow
Circumstances may cause directional pathways everywhere
Experiences make who we are when one guides here to there
Choices having to make not made from one second to another
Rather must pause to contemplate use your knowledge further

Nana mum son met ushering viewing an action play
A Hair musical spiced by dancing a sensuous gay
Never not forgotten etched in one mind's granite
This will only be lost last because all life is finite
How ever what is important to remember the fun
Old have many memories while young have just begun

Life is not destination or journey it is self epiphany
Existentially the individual forges their own destiny
Some dreams so allusive as leg swings to the next step
The course of a football game score when you have pep
Goals are always about your unique personality
Do not stop because of others words go consequently

Is there a reason for this today or an illusion
One realizes their own conscienceness conclusion
Memorizing all the lines of your soliloquy
Then dancing singing performing arts equally
So much of an inner joy elation is cathartic
Being training learning with family didactic

# Rust Colored Dreamscape

Realized I was climbing thru the back window of a school bus
There were no primary colors except just light beige to rust
Went to the middle walking down the aisle it was totally empty
Sat down put my arm on the top of the next seat dust a plenty
Looked out the windows on the other side everything light tan
Then a silent object went by speeding it was a moving van

As it went by it began to slow down and ran into low lines
The cab of the semi was all tangled up then saw the stop sighs
A man began to remove the light colored strings entwined
It took an eternity for the trucker to finally get it divined
Heard the motor on the rig get started and it pulled away
Thinking about what is happening decided not to stay

Stood and walked to the doorway stepped down to ground
Lifted my head to look the real colors were there all around
Consciousness startled me opening my eyes I had awakened
It was just a story traveling thru a dreamscape I just reckoned
Reflecting back into my subconscious it was an episode of sleep
Began trying to understand what images meant before bleep

When in the midst of the happening it seemed so unreal real
Analyzing the picture show did not have anything to feel
The rust color was that of old 1800's photographs of relatives
No people on bus symbolized aloneness and its derivatives
Entrapment of the big truck and resulting in its stopping
May have meant my position of stalled still just hoping

Very end it was a Wizard of Oz moment stepping into color
An awakeness into the next day different from the past flavor
Walking during the time kept thinking about the night's episode
Living breathing contemplating yet part still caught in the old
Breaking away from the past never really leaves the memory
Bits and pieces pasted together theme of the story contrary

Can not get rid of those fantasies during sleep time
Some things not even close to life like that paradigm
Wonder if there is something to be learned from extremes
A summation of all forgotten or remembered dreams
Again tonight am ready to cruise into that vivid land
Where what will be done uncomprehended not planned

# Taught Bigotry Vanquished

Flee your imposed life leave behind the heavy baggage
Emigrate to a far off thought to become a self savage
Can run away from false truth but it will find you
End to nothing boils to overflow when heart is blue
Realization you are your own self and become aware
Found entrance to the jungle and forge path to care

Taught the world was color shades of black and white
An empty pit in the gut signaled an unconscious blight
Not knowing why but understood something was wrong
Now looking back understand after siege finally gone
Must walk run the race by own foot steps to live a full life
Constantly hindered by bigotry hardships loss strife

Mask was lifted when parental servitude vanished
A veil lifted cleared the focus of why I was punished
My own singular beliefs were let loose to run free
Unbridled to think of what is right and should be
Self meditation concentrating on my inner being
Surfaced gasping for air to begin again thriving

It was not great leap of faith to become my own person
Found dread in patriarch grip because of persecution
Constant fang injection indoctrination to be them
Forged my trail with compassion to rid the problem
Began to travel in the fantasy illusions all my own
Seeking the answer of why we are here all alone

Witnessing from then on to create self into adulthood
Feelings around me many want to do bad not good
Surmising the many inequities of close pseudo friend
Traveling my own journey has been greatest dividend
Hell can be other people's imposing rejecting negative
However forged way thru the forest to reach a positive

Servitude in life is not to others thine own self be true
There's a point in young years to sever binding suture
Stop flow of propaganda to become your own person
Develop the sense of responsibility conscience reason
It is not necessary or is it to know what you have seen
Moving stopping understanding what is and has been

# The Lost Flower Song

The day mortal destiny fills body is the end of our existence
Consciousness fads to nothing we cease to possess providence
Fulfilled life which breathed every moment becomes object still
Greatest love your flower passes stem bends petal falls into rill
Silence pervades in the soul to cravenness depths unknown
A major part of your essence spread wings and has flown

Wake each day after restless night refuse she is gone forever
Hear a faint noise go to the next room hoping to be together
See chair next to the window think when will she come back
Thoughts accumulate behind dam no memories for to lack
Refute in mind that what has happened was meant to be
Wish she had not gone fast there was so much more to see

Begin to seethe inside that something so precious just went
Becomes like hot huge boiling cauldron steaming to vent
Inner fire produce fumes blinds reason why this happened
All functions shared in past gone any happiness dampened
Rage streaks thru the past histories that every life must go
Most cruel it is to be born live then told good-by amigo

Sorrow settles in heart break awakens the pain within
Try to lament swim against current still leads to chagrin
Some may say that all wounds heal with a passing of time
Injuries inside leave no scar and do not follow paradigm
Sometimes can not control how you feel about ultimate loss
Unable to regret that love which two held when hearts cross

Opened eyes melancholy has permeated muscles stay in bed
Nothing to get up for day free try to have more sleep instead
A vast sense it is only my sadness alone must just sing the blues
Dejection for what was now gone sombers emotions leads to rues
Darkness of rain cold fog lost in awakeness when be the doom
Past tracks walked over have become another person to loom

Been many years endured have swallowed all of the bitter
Never would she ever want me to end up just another quitter
Must yield once to the life forces and see grasp understand
Get back into the race flow and begin again sing in a band
Apt music follows always what heard is humming your song
Reach for a happiness continue to progress as you go along

# rhapsody

dreamscaping illusion not in
an awake state lighted up felt
ground spinning on daughters
merry go round do not stop
daddy with kaleidoscopic
bifocals on pony tail riders
up down around on the
draw bridge moving over
Styx river of fire by orange
gulls spiraling barely flapping
silent dam breached ripped
an opening seam squeezed
thru adjusting to light dim the
shades sight closed to see the
eyes opened reveal right in view
straight forward peripheral long
way to the end short cut non
existent melts the mortal soul into
glass metal rock alloy radioactive
disintegration sucked in by the
magneto into rainbow vortex
spinning passing c squared into
the white pin hole of brightness
transforming to non living ever
species existing on what is in the
cosmos cusp of consciousness

*Music is a higher revelation than philosophy.*
*Ludwig Van Beethoven*

# Chapter III
## circa MCMDXIX AD

*To sin by silence when they should protest*
*make cowards of men.*
*Abe Lincoln*

# The Flowers Are Gone?

Just a slave to the past,
Closing the gates behind fast;
Not looking back but only
with sick nostalgia.

Too many flowers have come
and gone, never to
be counted....but remembered.

The fragrance lingers as a dream,
And as the sun rises in
the skies of the
world, can there ever
not be what has been?

Never but when forgotten...
Lost at expense of that knowledge.

Oh! Whither away little
pedals, the autumn of
the years have come.
Think only of the sweet spring
which time will bring.
You will be remembered in time
Neither not less than now nor
when it was then mine.

Flowers fade away—
the memory is too
much, for one cares….

Rot and be lost—be gone:
no never will the
scent be blown away.

It is a wish—
could not come true.

A hope in the shadows.
Long will the time be
when those moments
are cast aside,
as this heart seeks a
place to hide.

The flowers grow again;
ocean waves continue:

the world never sleeps.

2 Apr

# Decadent Man

The pounding rhythm of single footsteps
walking down a vacant hallway,
is a sound to insolence
For random mobility human decay.

Ignoble of the pleasures and
joys brought by light.
And far less than nothing
when cometh the night.

Consciousness is the answer to the
question of living.
But in the land of want
there is no word like
giving.

Even the constant beat
is not the impetus for man.
I see the decadence as hypocrisy
and greed as an omen.

Fetal…
since the first light of dawn.
Dead…
when the last rays of sun have gone.

Do the steps suddenly stop or
fade away to nothing at the end?
It will be no consequence when it happens:
life will not begin again.

6 May

# My Dawn

At early light when birds sing
their minstrel notes,
Music comes out as repeats
of philosophic quotes.

The sky unchanged a placid
blue-gray,
Yielding to the passing time:
law of night & day.

How immortal these moments will be
when I forget and die.
Never gone, only passed like tears
from a mourners cry.

The trees turn green as
light ushers in the sun
And people wake to work
at jobs undone.

I hope this is the dawn
I've been waiting for.
The time I learn to be kind
And stop asking for anything
more.

28 May

For I have come a long way and have much
longer to go, if but to know one thing.
Letter Home

# Pathos of Life

I laugh at myself for mimicking
peoples' delusions,
While they that I mimic live lives
of frustration and confusions.

Crying out at flight
of the birds,
I wish selfishly to equal
truth with words.

I seek to know
but hide from learning,
And find each day
the fire still burning.

Everything will end sometime
and I'll have my corner to sit in.
A wasted life gone by
compared to those that win.

I will walk on in my simple
shell of demise
And leave the problems of the
world to the wise.

This is not how I would like
it to be
But that is the way things
end for me.

29 May

# 9 Jul 69

"I am what I am" to me
That is all I'll ever be.
Living in my world all alone
And knowing nothing that is known.

"I live in a world of my own"
only as far as I dream,
And walk many streets alone
tired as my feet may seem.
As reality sometimes crashes in
and a splash washes pictures away,
I realize my dreams could not have been
for I became less happy more each day.

Kisses can never leave the lips once kissed,
"Memories fade but are not lost."
And as the mind grows weak
the dreams of love are missed,
Thinking nothing of what the cost.

Search the rocky shores
and dive in the sea—
"What the heart longs to find
the eyes never see."

# CHOCOLAT-COVERED REALITIES

Everything I do is just a variation
of something else done,
And my life has already been lived
without regard to time.
For we all live in different dimensions
with thoughts only our own,
And die with self-secluded delusions
we have made all alone.

A vast anti-sphere engulfs
our minds and actions,
Leaving the world to revolve
around thoughts and reaction.
The mind will expand into infinity
and crush simple alternatives,
While those that must make a choice
will be ignorant of all dialogue.

Nothing can exist without the knowledge
of it's own existence,
And even then is assurance the
product of thought?
Simple theories sometime develop into
complex laws,
While mts of rock will someday
erode away to nothing.

We walk on the limits of the universe,
while our minds swim to the edge,
And talk about what is beyond
yet still not knowing all within.
We must fall until we have started
again to regain our
stupidity once more,
And reach only what we reached
so many times before.

11Aug

*Nothing is so easy as to deceive one's self,*
*for what we wish, we readily believe.*
*Demosthenes 349 BC*

# Remembered

Like a long arrow piercing my heart;
A piece of truth on an upward path…
Love is the leaves that fall in autumn
around trees.
The leaves and trees reflect
past love and love to come.

Let the leaf that falls to ground be an
inspiration to all things,
A life never ending in the nakedness of
a tree of the security of the ground.
As the bud of each new leaf begins
a bird sings,
And the summer blindness from the sun
holds us to his warmth.

The falling of leaves is a worship
of the autumn,
Watching each leaf as it lands,
is the end of an age.
Reach out and touch a leaf!
Remember the leaves in the winter…
enter a new phase…
Caught in the coincidence of thinking
leaves,
I can feel the love within my mind.
Gaining more than I lose…given thru

a recognition of what is--
My physic will reincarnate; fertilizing the
new with the old…
a life of a leaf…
An end to nothing

11 Nov

# Only Reality

What I think is only my reality
If that is a fantasy It is my reality of fantasy
I am finding out that what I think is so
What I want things to be are not so
The dream I had last night was my reality
No one else had the dream or my reality
The dream did happen in the sense of phenomenon
But it was a manifestation of my subconscious
Yet when I was having the dream it seemed real
As if I were awake and it was occurring consciously
So was my dream a reality to me?
The dream I experienced in my time
Dreaming is a reality when it is materializing
It makes no difference if it is true or false
When awake I think things from truth to falsity
That thinking is part of my reality
It has nothing to do with others realities
I can not perceive is what other realities are
I communicate with others by many methods
But no two can have the same realities only similar
No two can take the same steps in space & time
Each thought process is unique and unparalleled
For to be parallel presupposes two or more
And to be one can never to presupposed as two
One reality can be the same as another
My reality is my own as others are theirs
I can never know the realities of others
What is communicated to me can only be perceived
But perception is not exact reality by definition
The words that I write here is my reality to me
But what others think of it is not my reality

My words that others read can not be understood
Because the words I use are only symbols
My expression can vary as much as backward forward
And not knowing which direction is up or down
One has no reference point to start understanding
Realities are like ideas without any meaning to others
The concept of the existence of god could be put to a vote
Yes that there is No that there is not
But each within their own realities has no choice
A god is or is not according to one
It takes two to determine a choice
If one man existed and only one
That one person would have not choice
Their realities would be one
What they determined as truth would be
There would be no alternatives
Maybe in the beginning a choice was made
And once the choice was made no alternatives
It takes two words to distinguish true and false
with me god is one word no choice
God or nogod are words and choice
True or false are two words and choice
But I believe truth does not presuppose choice
The choice in a god has no alternative
Each one has their own truth
That part of a person where there are no alternatives
For some it is god others nogod
I am one and my truth is nogod
Those who oppose me have made a choice
Because to suppose or not is a choice
With purpose there is always selection

To make the choice presupposes alternatives
To have no alternatives there is no choice
To be truth there is no choice
My perception even deep is only the surface
Surface or a line in time infinity all around
Infinity of smallness & largeness is incomprehensible
There is only unending question for my mind
The only end conceivable is life and that may not be so
Yet to guess is not to know for sure
And only one thing is for sure—nothing is for sure
So, everything preceding this is conjecture
There are things that we have not control over
Other things we let happen when they could be altered
Things that should be changed and aren't are lost to change
The choice to change comes only once not twice
If a second chance comes around its not the first
There is only are first time the rest are that the rest
To know the difference between what and not to change
Wisdom is making the right choice the first time
But is to have choice the truth?
One goes through life doing things first never second
But choice is with every movement
To move, not to move seems all there is
Yet it would seem impossible to just not move ever
So to move is part of life with choice necessary
The choice is in the mind yet not philosophical
The philosophical choice is between volition & physics

*When the guns roar, the arts die.*
*Arthor Miller*

57

# Nostalgia

I was lying in my bed last night while the sun was going down and it brought back so may memories it hurt. Oh so long gone away into the past. Those summers of my boyhood when there was always something going on. It would be to warm to stay in and watch TV until darkness set upon grass. Sometimes the air conditioner would be on and you could watch a good movie or 'Mission Impossible", but generally it was the outdoors that gave the best invitation. Climbing the elm in the back yard to the upper most branches and looking out through the leaves to the sunset. To see the horizon I looked over the Red Cedar River Valley with the green of the trees like a carpet of soft leaf. Yes, I climbed that tree a lot just to be alone with myself and think. Once in a while I would take the binoculars up with me and follow the birds in flight or perched on some secluded limb. The sound of the martins was sometimes all I could hear up in the branches but the noise of man would always crash in every time.

On some summer evenings I would take off on my bike for no other reason than to be alone with myself and see nature. Riding through Bever Park with sun shining through the trees casting millions of shadows which seemed to be alive sometimes. Going in the other direction toward Neolridge Park there were less trees but you felt free with all the open space and sky. You can not imagine how it feels to think of those long rides out and back to the swimming pool. At times I would take off past Collins and ride the gravel roads a while, stopping every now and then to walk in the forest or down a dry creek bed. People looked at me like I was not there sometimes but they probably were not aware of what they were missing. I feel like running through an open wheat field in slow motion and then realize I have left the ground.

Of course when I touched down again my head would still be in the cotton clouds. That sight incomprehensible red-orange color of the sun going down over the horizon. I do not forget "...those lazy, hazy, crazy, days of summer..." back home. Someday if I return I'll probably look back with nostalgia on my US Army service too. 1969

# letgoholdon

amaneversomuchinexil
whenthoughtofwhatheisnot
peoplesorrythecastilehas
turnedtodustandblownaway
thisisnostereotypegoman
canonlybewhatheis
andnotwhatotherswant
movingtoaplaceothershavenotbeen
thesouloflifeistheultimatereasonforliving

# nothing

truth in the absence of belief is what you want it to be
time was when there was no man
to actually believe that we are different than things around us
only way to not have death is to not have life

from the idea of reality there could not be immortality
there is no choice or control over death or life
we are all only here when heart beats
there are no second chances

the past can not be changed, the present never stops
present is beyond the past and a moment away from future
there is only the between the beginning and the end
existence of matter is rearranged in relative space

all that really is?...
molecules changing to molecules
out side the intellect
there are only substances and their modifications

everything found will be lost
in the final analysis it does not matter what we think
thoughts can not be heard
only one thing is for sure. . .nothing

*Every one dies but not everyone lives.*
*A. Sachs*

# Chapter IV
## Quick Eternity

*Existence precedes essence.*
*John-Paul Sartre*

# Sound of Music

Piano fingers tingling soul of my heart
Dancing across ivory keys note chord
Tempo allegretto stoccado* Bach Mozart
To be heard by peon proletariat lord

Music the core of song from our being
Once it starts does not stop until ending
Lasting effects of emotional performance
Etched in memory forever remembrance

Stinging voice sparks titillation feeling
Accompaniment to fill aura inspiration
Two in concert with others passion seeing
Tis a ballet in the minds of concentration

Witness opera musical surrealistic
Performances show reality fantastic
Practice never seen by spectatories
Guided by soft strong hand mentors

The last act is the most dramatico
Aria bringing theme enlightenment
Final score Beethoven in crescendo
Seeing hearing such a delightment

*Rapier Thrust

# Last Love Song

My soul would rather be elsewhere to sing the last love song
Melody cascading kaleidoscopic vortex orbiting oblong
Know not where these inner feelings emanate lest my heart
Lips move with mind one step turning wheel to begin start

I disappear into the mist of uncertainty to search for Devonian
Life is only death of self illusion and a study into the oblivion
Ultimate demise is not without some large or small life lived
Embedded in awareness of a singular existence only believed

I will be gone when went have been past and final task done
Never to reach that apex of mountain top is not there is gone
No great river to be forged and reach that other green side
Last breath not even to be heard just ebbed out with the tide

The end is unconsciousness into unknown cavernous abyss
Others could not possibly understand or think to address
Abstract sentences just words spoken symbols untranslated
Decomposed compassion oozing from all pores unrelated

Invisible to eyes the sound is the last of my baritone voice
Leave loved ones behind when not by any or all a choice
Unaware those journeys or foot steps of others true being
Heart can not say what only that last love song feeling

# River of Love

Rain poured river breached levee
Emotions inside spilled over heavy
I danced the passion every dance
Then the heart pierced with lance

Light of darkness spreads across soul
Bring in feelings limbo takes a toll
Have in arms one next to you special
As hope comes goes landscape spatial

Live a walk the path of your self
Moments passed put on the shelf
Felt pain is in the mind not flesh
Days years do not dim the fresh

Tears come spontaneous blur eyes
What a real could have been dies
Cascading over cheeks descending
Gone lost realization of the ending

Eternity no exfoliation loss of love
Can never forget the flight my dove
When gone you can not bring back
Experience of touching being a fact

# Never Forgot

Left the pier sail to find life's meaning
Came back mind swimming dreaming
An energized search for level to attain
All on rough smooth silent noisy terrain

Loss moves one into loneliness grief
Holding that love not mere disbelief
Realize too at a time must let it go
Release relieve the now stressful tow

Only can go forward with next step
No going back yet the feelings kept
Walking our road travel a journey
Love somebody let go into eternity

My heart wants the question is what
Pursuit quest hedonism with chariot
Wheel turn toward epicurean type style
Just to be but alive here a short while

Amazement to see flight of your dove
Special dance no end to a shard love
Once forever so lucky total happiness
The pristine part of two soul's closeness

# Phantom Earth

Man's increased burning of fuel producing carbon dioxide
Facilitating mass water molecules in the clouds to ride
Saturated atmosphere eventually releases rain in torrent
Record down pours from thunderstorms at any moment

Many more humans heating in cold cooling in heat
Vast industrialization production commodities to meet
Deforestation a devastation to the balance of oxygen
Changing natural hydraulic machine in every region

No more hunting gathering cultures to balance nature
A maximum growing technology employed to nurture
Price equates to green lined pockets of an entrepreneur
Let the next generation deal with fate we have no fear

Ice capes glaciers snow melting seven seas on the rise
All low land masses are submerging what a surprise
Earth has become an over populated Petri ecosystem
Fast approaching catastrophic Agamemnon cataclysm

It has become apparent the process is irreversible
The now time is all that matters to the insatiable
Civilization has never matured and is declining
Scientific evidence is so clear there is no denying

# Embryo Existence

To walk alone high on a hill at sundown
Heart wanders to find that not ground
Feelings of what others have felt for me
No reverse stream lives ever remain to be

Can not take away sadness lost from eye
Living world surrounded hello goodbye
Friendships here until the end is in sight
Shadows creep slowly past hope dim light

Brightness of flames will out last fuel
Embryo remembrance birth renewal
Turn off the mind at our last breath
Leave with others down existing path

Next moment always seems come slow fast
Yesterdays can only multiply into the past
Reality impossible to erase a grief found
Any destination will no longer be bound

Sense of joy fills with knew introduction
Shadow within memory comes a question
Aloha could become tomorrow experience
Perhaps a smile consciousness existence

*A real work of art is like a dream, for all its apparent obviousness*
*it does not explain itself and is never unequivocal.*
*Carl Jung*

# Silent Quick

Want to remember parts of memory
Forget oh many the episodes dreary
No erase takeaway discretionary past
Just a human brain crass to the last

A moment in time is only once
What passes by reality experience
Leaves fall from a tree gravity
Seed germinates up levity irony

Run silent when thinking deep
Swim smooth and feather your feet
Then can ponder what beyond infinity
Imagine warp speed entering futurity

Saw what appeared to eyes be illusion
Thought a second turned into delusion
A consciousness feeling comprehensible
Next instant an aura of unpredictable

Holding onto the last breath
How a growling that is trick
Born living ending in death
Not knowing life gone so quick

# *Apart From*

Motion moves along beginning end
So life of living is from birth to rend
Everything knowledge between black white
Our space in time only a flash of light

Single segment time continuum infinity
No choice at all in eventual finality
Can not live past just thought memory
Only time to love comfort friend family

Tears can not hide pain behind eyes
Living is surrounded hello good byes
Different times same people want
Sing dance try to revive the pant

Past gone except the feelings in memory
Now always realize caught in summary
Search for reason meaning being here
None ultimate intellect that can hear

Rode a river barge into the lock
Mississippi ride from dock to dock
Aim to focus inward to soul heart
Thought outward to realize apart

# Beyond Reach

There was a moment our four eyes met
All inner emotions realized silent kept
Body turned away to dance the next set
Memory only to go be gone when has left

Gait those cross steps talk a mini speech
Never not focused on primordial search
Round the floor in music stance cadence
Brings ethereal soui into a whirl of sense

Face to face existence in the now season
Stretch boundaries reaching for reason
Most of us thrive not without food water
Think more less reduces flesh to matter

Life's pictures are more than word
To touch felt like rasp sharp sword
Sincere hugs embrace memorisms
Every smile goes beyond aphorisms

Alas what one strives to conquer
Dissolves into the abyss of squalor
Fantasy what an individual want
Erased air by life that we can not

# Life Hesitation

Rose real early to just gaze the star
Look between into the darkness afar
Wondering in mind meaning infinity
Reach grasp my soul lives into eternity

Road walked destiny with each step
Time into future some memories kept
Come to realize fact knowing nothing
Experience like that of lost love ring

Harmony calls being seek understand
Epiphany path the moment heart rend
Where do we go from this false here
Live a choice stay with thought bear

Reach core there is no veer brash
Silence broken when happen splash
No map where all ride destination
Awakenings well up with hesitation

Thought gone where there reason
Conscious life an illusion version
Journey complete a mere pretence
True ideal that was never existence

# Regal Dream

Presence of Queen lips soft eye loveliness
Word spontaneous exude consciousness
Floating the wave in an ocean of honey
Top of sweetness never to leave memory

To be or not to be in love nay choice
Truth has no mask alternative voice
Second lost when not take opportunity
In the air efflorescence of profundity

Only deep compassion is body of a soul
Without heart reduced chunk of coal
Space between two minds is constant
Far what self wants can be a distant

Existence once think conceive enlightenment
A spirit moves the body toward self fulfillment
Past at heel live now future beyond step of toe
Passion wind moon happen whence tomorrow

Regal only when stoop to help a child
Dream some occasion dare to be wild
Have fantasy presentation of a tiara
Experiencing their happiness aura

# Life Between

Truth absence of belief what wanted to be
Time was there were no sapiens to see
Think we different than life presence
Only way to not pass is non existence

An idea of reality non immortality
There choice control death living
All here when we have mortality
Chances not freely a giving

All that really is known atoms
Molecules changing to molecules ions
Outside the intellect incomprehensible
Inorganic elements their improbable

Beyond the second away to future
Body just product of nature
Past nonchangable present no stop
The living is between beginning end pop

Everything found will be lost
Analysis no matter what thought toast
Soul can not be heard lest you sing
Only one thing is for sure...nothing

# Destination Eternity

lean down slope into the snow
ski to a destination do not know
fly soar face into the wind sky
feel the rush of molecules go by

ever a time once to be self
falling down the steep cliff
turn around this way that
contemplate where soul is at

grasp that reality for just a moment
release inner imagination to ferment
moment in a special time felt fervent
next second is only there when present

never catch that which can not be caught
when in midst life always state of doubt
try to answer a question which is sought
reason human life not purchase bought

life loss gain see it in stock market
happiness walks on a different carpet
progress through portal to epiphany
ever the approaching pseudo eternity

*I don't seek, I find.*
*Pablo Picasso*

# Chapter V
## Dream Hope

*The dream is a disguised fulfillment of a suppressed wish.*
*Sigmund Freud*

# Odorless Feces Unfiltered

The future is behind me entirely gone forever
Dreams oxidized in to hydrogen atoms dispersing
Redevelop subconscious movies to awake illusions
Fall forward into history fiction meaninglessness

The next step is the most important of life
Now is not end to consciousness being
Now piercing into near distant delusion
Daily infusion awareness pulse throbbing

Must embrace what I grasp to freely think
Imprisoned thought is not self reality allusion
Each life is theirs to live wholly uniquely
Flying across mindscapes like clouds going by

All I have is this moment to breathe breath
Using brain to realize I am here this second
Life is way to short to think backward forward
Just living from heart beat to heart beat

Mosey on down the road to see the world
Through the forest over the hill and rill
Smile on my face reminiscing of the good times
Wanting to make knew memories to cherish

# Path Foot Step

want that which is impossible to have
climb and never reach the top
run and not get there
dream and none come true
lost friendship many a reason

bridges crossed can not be uncrossed
chances lost…lost forever
passion consumed by time
leave emotion imprisoned
smoldering beneath subconscious

moment in love…moment next
still in love…hand on breast
air of the night a breath
in the energy of real lust
memory of lips unseparated

temptation morphs psyche
creates fools in outward
hope to survive with others
descending the steep grade
looking up to finish on high note

# Life Purpose Be Compassionate

If you are not chasing life with goals to attain
Complacency sets in to rue and think the profane
Being is more than just existing rather all that is ever
Down from high horse up from despair an endeavor
Not going for full potential wasting chance is bane

Time to race run away face inevitability sail the yacht
Depends on outlook self strength what was taught
Living no choice then evolved to everything is choice
To stand in rain and tell it like it is with you voice
Defines ones personally to rise and accept your lot

End of life is when one realizes early decisions primal
Make wrong turns follow others making life dismal
Take the reins of heart and move to where that place
It could be most anywhere should be your happy space
Make direction where more like you just to be normal

Apparent horizon existence one experience perception
Traveling over rainbows listing in a sea of deception
Deviating from the wants needs that encompass self
Your ship launched to take you over flat earth shelf
Cascade to the other side reaching to your perfection

Barefoot walking to reach over the hill to paradise
Along the path one must deal with and pay the price
Not individual gratifications the strife worthy purpose
Bringing to focus ethical values away from morose
The very end to all things be compassionate and nice

*The world is but a canvas to the imagination.*
*Henry David Thoreau*

# Seek To Dream

one can only talk to those with deaf ears
however does it matter they understand
the many can not make me wise foolish
for others do not care about the now
either know or void of having feeling

they who fight for right must do it on own
no one mandated to yield from reprisal
search inner to seek virtue and wisdom
never mind private interest invaders
game only appears happy when won

opposites are generated out in of each other
ideally excluding one from the chosen
exhibit patience as pleasure follows pain
voice of conscience reminds of good
that none are innocent lest challenged

when spared verdict of death
feeling that one lives forever
life journey is about to avoid
uprightness runs swifter that feet
kill to stop censure of evil mistaken

not unconscious a dreamless sleep
changed migration to another dimension
what torture to be immortal
with those aberrant now
dare to dream is all in the moment

# In Love

Walk together on a forest trail in the rain
Fog slowly consumes our space
Hold hands running on white sand into surf
Held dance spin embrace and look into eyes
Conversation ebbing a moon waxing
Spicy song resonates to fill the ambience
Aria fills the soul body twist of fate
Remembrance exuberance noninsignificance
Never not forgotten when in your arms today
Gone as far as now yet maybe tomorrow

Constant time continuum in all life
Take the moment to reflect reject in calm
Next step comes goes love etched in stone
A meteor star an image across sky
The flash of light retina optic chiasma
Can not run fast enough to catch nothing
What is gone only lost to the past
To rein as king would be insult to peon
Pure conscience embodied in heart
Sunset orange espied two snuggled in blanket

Can see another time place realize this
Never comprehend others thoughts
Surmise maybe yet have doubts
Deltoid flex sludge clever wedge split
Hearth heat primordial sapien existence
Survival day dream human essence
Other side of existence extinction
Feel the hurt of having no pain
Superficial yet some damaging felt
Majic happening escapes the fringes

Hold on to that which deep into
Speak forked tongue only viper
Honor can be amidst honourable
Cross crevasse under duress feeling
Last is still what it has always been
What I know is to just chase the blues
One can listen to the music voice whisper
Ever felt love immersed encapsulated
Wasted time in that one moment gone
Only a breath could have changed forever

The night was right but it did not happen
Cause to dance again never more
Celebrate what we had at a time
Ethereal non plastic encompassed in
Hence can dream you holding me
Surrealistic hallucinogenic vestige
Have not changed the heart beat is done
Farewell to those gone just living loving
Complacent to the end of what ever
Walking sleeping feelings till none

# Sandman Lost My Love

Sandman sent me a dream last night
Found myself climbing mountain alone
Then dense fog came rolling up the cliff
Lost sight and could not find the way
Realized my search for love was gone

Having that stupid sorry for my lot feeling
Then I saw some one who was blind living
Alive better than me must have lost my focus
Felt that dumb pride not good for any body
Stubborn no one to help me could not just ask

Sleeping the awake dream that is my reality
Conscience is my numbness felt tomorrow
Surrounded by what thought that is not there
Brain marrow oozing into a conscious blight
Found serenity in mid air landing of terror

Lights seen on the ground flying thru mind clouds
One can see in the darkness that bright light erases
Seeing flat of a needle tip as big as desert mesa
Without the two where is the reference point sight
Smile then go inward to makes ones self happy

As strong as the holy rusty bucket is weak
Running across tight rope under the rainbow
Could not get there faster to the no pot of gold
Found multiple holes in memory not to be restored
All lost to the lot forgotten unremembered love

# See the Unseen

As a sapiens was brought up indoctrinated to feel special
Top of the food chain evidence that we have superior brain
So for all of the words are symbols understood by only few
To feel better than other life is a learned interpreted perception
And as I think that in the scheme of life we are different

The only thing we really have is consciousness as we just live
What one does with that window in time defines who we are
Does it really matter into posterity that will end for everybody
Man will not last very much longer as we know it whether at all
So many want to make the most of what they have regardless

Others believe that there is an after life and prepare for theory
There are those who do not know what life is but poverty & food
It is sad to see those so rich to not want to share with those poor
Contrast between greed hate despair is man's fault ultimately
Humanity's end is certain because we will never go any where

Natural resources are running out with no hope to get more
Population will increase in size that will become unsustainable
Pollution will become so toxic it will not be reversible ever
People can not comprehend the vastness of what everything is
All are running down a dead end path ending unknowingly

Some know but few that this unbelievable idea as actual truth
If one looks at the total of factual data it would be apparent
It may seem this to be a fatalistic theory that appears insane
However signs are everywhere one looks with mass disasters war
What will probably happen is the sun will explode end of life

We could be sucked into the vortex of a super nova black hole
Reducing every molecule atom to hydrogen proton electron
To not grasp this concept would seen to be naïve and gullible
Feelings that are lost now without trying to live is foolhardy
Hope is the only thing to make it to the end as best one can

# Compassion of Hearts Empathy

Nation of being human ununique one who was brought
Mind war games not our own far away from a thought
Wrestling those inner demons we have built outward
Protection by method deployed by psyche a said word
Lost in a blizzard a firing of flares can not be taught

Youth found nothing experienced what did no plan
Less than little just animosity false help from clan
Finally realized the any one to count on is be self
Mislead to quicksand side line laughing dismal felt
Found inside following heart became no also ran

Soaring to high an epiphany to care for me first
Built up inside empathy compassion ready to burst
Looking to the less fortunate and take under my wing
Cradled their woes helped the blight with song to sing
Anything worth fighting for that is good can not be worst

Dedication to those who really need the warmth of a hug
Personality put down at every stop sigh swept under the rug
Best to be there when they are in the most ever of your need
Can not sacrifice anything when blind to those who bleed
It can not be within a big heart to look away and shrug

When in the middle of mid stride of when able to give
One must donate more than money feel love to help poor to live
No name on a monument will turn into food for the starving
To witness the rich flaunting while them are not surviving
A heart longs to feel the mind yields to a passionate relative

# Visceral Passion

Life is not about being the best
But living doing your best every time
It is the loses most remembered
Can make one better or wallow in self pity
Ripples of words in stream of thought
Destination varying with current in a dream
Change is something can never be same
Only all what have is coming going
Seen seldom what actually seem
Living what a travesty end mortality
Cost of treason of soul eventual agony
Fool over and ever confirm humanism
Grief remembrance a crevasse unknown
All powerful leads to another ruse
Words can not explain lost horizons over hill
Where is home house earth universe being
To help someone in need changes your life
There is the letter of the heart
There is the intent of the heart
There are those who have none
Others it just beats and does not
Examine consciousness
Does not give of self or wealth
Does not care about the children starving
Very few are at the top of pyramid
Compassionate ones
Ones who have conscience
Opens it up to the world

It can not be taught
Yet learned or not from parents and culture
Some must find their own way or follow
Make mistakes and know what they are
To change one way or the other
Suffer or reap the consequences
Though be poor of wealth rich with passion
Came thru slave like youth to survive
Arrive strong with resolve
Still tortured by acquiescence of moments
Took sanctuary in homage with deference
Never best worst by virtue me
What to do others know of after life
Has no meaning for me
All alone now exist with creatures
Plunging into the final abyss

# Sympathy

remember the happy times with sad tears
by gone moment to grasp carry
close to heart
friend came went as a river
so too mountain vista tempest torrent
one determines what important not
foci of an equilateral isosceles
vena cava essential not without aorta
gravity both moon revolving not spinning
tides ebb flow earth rotating
nuance of human life experience
existential to the individual
no feet can step in the same space
some perish for vernacular expression
what do you hold let go to oblivion
meditate to center of soul
expand mind to optimum consciousness
word meaningless when no comprehension
thought is of volition
in life we do not feel death nothing
reality is personal privacy pondered
living in dream miles away
fate evolving as we think
awake the world has changed
believe what want have been went
a mission make own trail to walk
speak self truths inside out
to challenge what is wrong is right

light of a candle can brighten a cavern
a twinkle in an eye may alter mood
live beside yourself for company
loyalty is honor with purpose
sympathy is highest form of compassion

*...dream structures are, as it were, lifted above the floor of our*
*mental life and float in psychical space like clouds in the sky,*
*scattered by the first breath of wind.*
*Adolph Strumpell*

# Chapter VI
## Soldier Patient Volunteer

*The unexamined life is not worth living.*
*Socrates 399 BC*

# Civilization Never Matured

Waiting for the one letter not wanting it to come came
You are drafted into the Army welcome to the war game
Girl friend stunned drops you like an unwanted photo
Seems the far killing fields need their newspaper promo
Fat old geezers push naïve young life into their grave
Sacrificing everything can for their homestead to save

Physical taken pledge oath flight to next destination
Some hesitate whether to go to Canada not a question
Being unable to swim you were dropped into pool of fire
No doubt you were the anonymous number wanted for hire
Initial experience of break down build up brain wash
Just becomes natural after basic a mother photo op flash

Cadence learned obstacle course field first aid not infantile
Advance infantry training march high rifle non stop twelve mile
Daily dozen predawn calisthenics double time in formation
Ten pull ups mess door eat breakfast just a military operation
Firing LAWS Rocket 45 pistol bazooka M50 tossing hand grenades
Our fire works were ground explosions orange napalm no parades

Secure gear step into the door soar 'Airborne All The Way'
Land tree branch water splash ready with M16 main stay
Friends do come and go fox hole buddies etched in soul
We are fighting for all peoples freedoms no matter the toll
Parasites Agent Orange eating flesh away to the bone
Protect the platoon even if you are one standing alone

Rain patrol into VC controlled night movement extremely slow
Claymore mine trip wire precaution in pitch black no moon glow
Monsoon for weeks twenty four hours soaked to core nothing dry
Think of those home loved ones living in freedom no room to cry
Tour of duty over war not done still bound for US land I love
Loss of dignity insanity inhumanity have appreciation of dove

Returning to my town in uniform shunned spat upon oh! Why?
Must be those living in their cozy brick houses wanted us to die
Vietnam slowly fades away unknown to most not those who served
America will never realize the honor of our courage deserved
I stand at attention tall in the face of any egregious force
Truly hoping that in the future nothing will happen worse

[Author trained for Vietnam but never went]

*An unjust peace is better than a just war.*
*Marcus Cicero 43 BC*

# Second Battlefield Medic

Erected in 1949 VA hospital vibrant heart that throbs with Hero life
Health issues scars seen invisible old age
consequence nation in strife
The second battlefield holds onto dreams of family living a happiness
Sun rising hundreds travel miles to receive care for past righteousness
Parked my car truck van rode shuttle cart bus to visit monolith in sky
Entered awed guided by informational ambassadors a place to rely

You have become a some one to be cared for important an individual
Wait at sign for clerk aid nurse PA doctor observations data residual
Then referred to radiology bone density
CAT scan MRI technician experts
Walking shorts jeans slacks brown green
suit tie lab coat Police blue skirts
Wheel chair crutches walker gurney limp
prosthesis movement atmosphere
Volunteers red vest directional passing
oxygen canisters rolling IVs appear

Cafeteria prepared dinner short order burger
fries custom hero spinach wrap
PX no tax clothing belts TV's candy bars socks
sodas shirts thongs appropriate
The quiet chapel mediation a wedding Sunday
service singing chaplains care
Social workers patient advocates an Ethics
Committee advance directives DNR
Electric doors granite floors elevators to a
basement blood draw up to the 10th
Traverse yards miles multiple appointments
up around then back next month

NEWS at the heart ground first floor north
east west south hallways direction
Signs on walls arrows right left codes red fire
blue medical green confrontation
Silver mail shoot runs down email sent escort
call pick up mail go to mail room
Audiology hearing loss of artillery rifle fire
grenade bomb loud injurious boom
Windows are the port holes to out side green
tree top carpet church spires blue sky
Parking ramp construction UI buildings
football stadium helicopters land fly

Research and Health Committee subjects
all NIH grants to annual approval
The collaborations resulting in life saving
forefront techniques ever so novel
Test thymusectomy of induced cancerous
T-cells exposed to cesium radiation
Trials replicated brought positive cutting
edge cure technology titration
What holds us together when things fall apart
spouse friends strong willed body
Minds of people trained what they want to
do to help you in times of quandary

Rheumatology oncology bone marrow biopsy
histology analysis pathology
Dermatology psoriasis dialysis infusion
confusion release information urology
The rare only veteran's infectious diseases
vast antibiotic regiments' treatment
Health Vet allergy podiatry the foot steps
are the way to parking lot cement
Instinctual genetics follow intuition again to
see pyrotechnics over the rainbow
Only up to your singular existence to learn
what the mind needs wants to know

# Eye Clinic Waiting Room

Went to the animal hospital two leggeds where everywhere
Walking standing sitting talking looking around
As they pass by each smell is different sweat to perfume
Sometimes there is silence and noise comes in from outside
Can not sit to long bottom sweats muscles stiffen

The cause for most being here is eye sight health
Without being here would mean blindness of sense
Quality of life is diminished to a state of debilitation
Permanent condition person will need to adapt and overcome
Temporary with care to get back to normal is hoped for

100 years ago I would be blind with this problem
Modern methods enable one to have hope to be whole again
Life expectancy has increased so to physical break downs
Living with a nutritious mind set helps reduce ailments
Exercising to the entire body helps to cope with what comes

Waiting allows one to actualize their unique being
Going forward moves you into the next moment
Arriving to meet a stranger joke teller deaf to your voice
Enjoyed camaraderie caring for another's stories life
With out others we may not be here dependant on self

Think you are coming to the end of a visit not
Look around comers and goers time is passing slowly
Smiles frowns blank faces sleeper's lookers
All peoples with their own thoughts feelings aims
Alas the days' page is done to rest for the next day

It rains when conditions are right for falling moisture
Sunshine during day when clouds do not cover the sun
Thoughts drive into awareness most times for thinking
Delving into what is is not not for consumption
Occasionally ideas will not leave the picture show

The projector is on to tell a story explain an issue
Feelings enter to give a perspective to what is not
Overwhelming the neuro pathways running self
To over loading can cause a circuit malfunction
A blown fuse resulting in darkness of the transmission

My foot hurt then I saw one with no leg
Arm ached then helped a man with no arm
In for eye surgery saw a man that was blind
Thought how dumb I am heard some one speech impaired
Walked with a sore hip got passed by a wheel chair

Living my life found out a friend had passed
Complained about the fast drivers got behind some one slow
Barely walked down the hallway looked out to see joggers
Was in the store full basket there a mother with food stamps
Could not go to sleep heard a guy had to work double shifts

Felt I was smart ran into an old professor
Could not wait to get home went by a homeless begging
Realized I was past my prime talked with a 96 year old
Retired from working as the next workers filed in
Thought I was moving slow a snail came slimming past

Thank you Eye Clinic Personnel

# Volunteered Yesterday

Yesterdays keep adding up, waking daily
to face small eternity in the next step
Blink to sun light on brow, experiences of past
tucked away in the memory bytes
Dress for the weather, agenda to follow,
Head into the destination wanted
down hill level up around then park
Doors open see those who cross my path
some are robotic in facial façade
going to their place they must be
wishing they were somewhere else
Adjust to others a natural smile my constant given
Walk hall ways a glimpse of Shelby smile maybe today
Up down elevator for hours some are empty box cars
others evolve into memorable conversations
Proud to ware the red vest a badge of courage
Ambassador soldier serving with honorable others again
This time there no enemy in cross hairs only friends
their disease is my quarry, to assist the best I can
each one is different some with child a bag to give
On wheels limping tapping blind stick all equal to me
if they need help getting some place they are taken


The purpose for being alive is what I am doing today


There is no ending of the times only the next day
Looking forward to the adventure of being with peers
Will arrive tomorrow when it comes, enjoying the smiles
hand shakes winks nods, glad what I am doing
Something that can not be taken away from me
a massive cathartic injection into my small soul

No better feeling than having endorphins well up
maybe not lasting long but ever self remembered
Precious archives of this single heart that does care
It is not the many hours of time spent together rather
relationships, building friends in a common ideal
A veteran just helping Veterans in the same fox hole

# Quintessence Met

When we met said if younger I would hit on you
My woman had passed and I just was feeling blue
You jokingly replied if older you would hit on me
We both knew with exchanged smiles us not to be
You have someone I none but memory of serene years
Before loss we had wonderful bless did not shed tears

So nice to have someone acknowledge my existence
Coming going up down elevator smoke scent presence
An arm touch to feel alive again not inappropriate
Nothing in this alone mans life to relate or equate
Cathartic to have non relationship contact pretend
Extraneous two five days pseudo acquaintance friend

Dreamscape awake is walking illusion thinking
Sleeping subconscious taps fantasy eyes blinking
Delving into my history of feelings deep long past
Memories bringing those gone away ever so vast
It is the good times that well up that I so now see
Ignorant as always to the thing not meant to be

I still have to continue breathe air and believe
Deal with cards dealt me even though I grieve
To round the next corner in hospital hall way
Christmas morning eye surgery most any a day
Always was a pleasure to witness your hi there
If to never speak again not forgotten you care

*Too often we underestimate the power of a touch a smile,*
*a kind word, a listening ear, an honest compliment, or the*
*smallest act of caring, all of which have the potential to*
*turn a life around.*
*Leo Buscaglia*

# Chapter VII
## Iowa City Press Citizen

*Our liberty depends on the freedom of the press, and that cannot be limited without being lost.*
*Thomas Jefferson*

# Insidious Floods

A world bread basket from succotash fields of beans and corn
Feeding also nematodes root worm porcine bovine Iowa born
Blessed with moisture in our latitudinal temperate zone
Cursed by droughts tornadoes high winds and hail stone

Floods eventually come when merciless heavy rain pours
Those in the river plain have water come through their doors
Engineers plan means of protection from nature's scourge
Only to relent when beat by a vast power and might surge

Reservoir dam to hold back many rivers volumes in place
Knowing with architectural wisdom built an overflow space
Levees are mounded rip rap stacked yet ultimately a breach
Then a flash torrent lifting carrying things to a new beach

Aftermath milieu of tempest is devastation and carnage
Lives homes heirlooms gone for some the high cost is savage
Scars will stay with the victims psyche the rest of existence
Some hope this will just be a once in a life time experience

# Turn of the Wheel

RVs trucks trailers buses cars bikes on top
Came to our neighborhoods for a night stop
Rest and relax their strongest of muscle heart
After an evening of culture next day do depart

A life moment only happens but once
To seize the day Carpe Diem existence
Meet strangers now make a difference
Never a second out of your experience

Helmets go by on many wheels turning
The knee feet legs are up down churning
Stand watch waving as magnitudes pass
Wonderful to feel joy you see in the mass

What a pearl in the Corridor agenda
Souls are here from across America
Rode in on one day saw conquered
A great happening ever remembered

Register's Annual Great Bicycle Ride Across Iowa

# Half orange

Woke eyes closed coming out of dream kaleidoscope
supine on living room couch
covered with white sheet soft pillow

Opened lids sight in darkness
moon glow light of cream colored curtains
it must be four the time I wished to wake

Sat up twisted waist slipped toes into thongs rose
walked over fringed ornate Persian rug
open front doors to cool morning air

Step out and down to stoop then again to driveway
went thru Linden tree shadow to view whole clear sky
then appeared a half full orange moon

The predicted lunar eclipse

Mind shot millennium straight to ancient aborigines
how did they then explain what I know
still beauty of vast changing cosmos

# Card Game

Trump is Clubs....beating primordial drums
awakening fervor in nation's heart
Political rhetoric moves forward and evolves
with the next throw of the dart

Listen to ponder the real issues a windmill in your mine
Truth is not choice a decision is hard to determine
November feels so far off to what will happen
Facades barricades expounding lips flappin

Caucus system again is contested who will be first
Tradition continues for the moment quenched thirst
Disproportionate cost to the we the people
Rock splash in pond causing increasing ripple

On election day it is an end and a beginning
Wish hope for best in our future now starting
Host of platitude speeches roared
Post vote all said agenda ignored

Anger cast but not with a stone
Let our freedom smile be shown
What ever has been said is gone
Hand off baton within comfort zone

Race competition has final moment
All is erased every last comment

A poem for the election

# Compassion

ponder the shadows now

minion amidst just bourgeoisie

each mere person counts

when dirty wash hungry feed

to stoop help a compassion

turn away no option

beauty in everyone to find

life force is the only thing

orphanage loss for ONE

love rushes to eyes seen

your legacy is inconsequential

embrace feelings of empathy

gift of heart never taken away

caring not a necessity innate

hold on to that dear

*What wisdom can you find that*
*is greater than kindness?*
*Jean Rousseau*

# Forever Valentine

There no special day
when in love

To those every moment
nothing to prove

Kiss hug morning night
ever a delight

Never core feeling doubt
out of sight

Roses delivered message
on a card

Most feel it is a required
standard

Appreciate each day with
your one

Better than standing
singular all alone

Sincere caring innate
quality of heart

Cant fool soul with pseudo
false start

Be together in your love
to live forever

Shroud over anything
transparent cover

Time is not less more
when deepest

Being with mate surreal
gale tempest

Smile is only skin touching
so tactial

Mind gray matter
reaching for theatrical

Hold on to what you have
tight
    Keep eyes open blinking in
sun light
    Squeeze    softly    until
turning azure
    Realize the person next
to you true

# Remember: Freedom is never free

As we approach the real Memorial Day which is
150 days from the first of the year,
let us all as American citizens be mindful of what it truly is.
It is a day set aside to honor all of those 1.4 million who have
lost their lives on the battle fields of war for the
freedoms we enjoy in this country today.
Most celebrate by vacationing on the Monday before and spend it
without thought of the many brave souls long forgotten.
It was born during the good time for flowering plants
around the battleground cemeteries after the Civil War.
Soldiers' graves were decorated by the southern (Gray)
soldier's wives, mothers, sisters and daughters.
They became moved and also honored the graves of the northern
(Blue) soldiers, knowing their families were grieving as well, far away.
At President Abraham Lincoln's Gettysburg, Pennsylvania
cemetery address of 1863 he said, "We cannot forget."
This referred to the nearly 1 million who had perished during
the bloodiest war in human history that pitted brother against
brother and father against son. It was that sentiment that
inspired Gen. Logan to issue an order to the Grand Army of the
Republic to decorate the graves of all soldiers lost in battle.
Memorial Day was first officially observed on May 30, 1866.
But today's Memorial Day is more than that. We
honor all veterans who paid the ultimate sacrifice
from the Revolutionary War to the present.
The words of President Thomas Jefferson are as true today
as they were during the Civil War and the birth of this nation
when the Declaration of Independence was signed.
"The tree of liberty needs to be watered from time to
time by the blood of patriots and tyrants," he said.

So if we as a country do not educate our youth why lives were sacrificed for the cause of their freedom, then generations yet to come are destined to make the same mistakes. Freedom will never be free.

*What you have experienced, no power on earth*
*can take it from you.*
*Viktor Frankl*

# Chapter VIII
## Precious Others

*Our life depends on others so much that at the root
of our existence there is a fundamental need for love.
Dalai Lama*

# The Kiss

Rose to greet Venus appearing
Stars still the earth spinning
Eminent light of sun glows
Human day sound of crows

Closed eyes to see opened blind
The journey life quest to find
Reach grasp hold which dear
Life nothing if not kind with fear

A path dream gone figment fantasy
Left unconsciouscy reality translucency
One learns shunned by commonality
Finds strength power enduring familiarity

Walked to the mountain eroded away
Searched my soul here to stay
Went to river felt earth living moving
Looked skyward saw vultures circling

Closeness intimacy what a time
Feeling of surrealistic paradigm
To realize the past in memory
A Kiss lips touching sincerity

# Heart of Soul

Nothing taken away when solid in heart
Know spirit soul not gone never to depart
Human is to live learning to be kind
Deep within the crevices of your mind

Adrift in an endless sea only darkness see
Descending into abyss thinking this is life to be
Intelligence without light hope is blindness
All that is are the treasured seconds of bliss

A person comes into life that defines yourself
Precious memories until consciousness gone
Rainbows shared vistas at the edge of a cliff
Never for a moment the love with me alone

Person can not go back to the once it is
Past is premise to future life in a presence
Emotion width breathe when love past existence
No one else can feel that when up to bat his

Could there be an ever compassionate lass
I can not compare to she was such princess
While some sit in their eternal apathy
Naïve served loyally my love ever faithfully

# Statuesque Memory

Reminisce as those memories flood away
Perceive the withered flower of yesterday
Fallen petal on ground as life within flies
The destination of promises turned to lies

Thought love would last now it is gone went
What could have been was only mind dreamt
Came from wishing for ended a morose heart
Living my life in constant phase of false start

Nostalgia of precious moment never dwindle
It is a lasting thought past never to rekindle
With that feeling existing every placid day
Perpetually there within what I do and say

There are so many regrets to shape and hold
A memory of all those times and places of old
No more ever to see the statuesque on display
Another journey to find happiness some day

Farewell to that beauty with freckled breast
Forever love still inside yet completely at rest
Raised eyes once more to the sun in the west
Survive love again and be in a state of quest

# Bright Reflection

complacent the world may seem
even moods change with seasons
and we play with own emotions
always asking the question why

as if to satisfy inflated egos
to create illusions in deeds
pass the dream and enter reality
when the body seeks vital needs

how many miles must we walk
before the ultimate end is found
it is that one infinite decimal
to which mankind is bound

bright fire reflections of light
keep us from a darkness of night
practicing winged man in flight
has seemed an unending plight

pebble piercing a pool of water
ripples move outward diminishing
blurring the pictures of the world
embedded in the cortex of mind

# Choice Here Gone

Heart chooses brain has no say when enter love
Permanent a sickness one can not avoid ever
Try to keep it when she flies far away forever
Some feelings deep stay in the soul a life time
Like a great song using only the good notes

Losing the way when on a journey to find happiness
Can be a rough road when light can not be seen
Walking in the darkness becomes a normal event
Getting used to what the is probably inevitable
One finds in self that happy place and enjoys

Not jumping delight but relish moment found
To hold on tight that which is most dear
Time stands still to last frozen in the mind
A brazen choice to be who when tomorrow now
Stepping on the dirt of earth being until not

Listening to sound going coming ending starting
In blindness squinting to see a spark life beam
Finding that which wanting mostly impossible
Discovering new territories are to reach out to
Having nothing everything are illusions lived with

Thoughts that pass by not stopping into the gone
A released latent response is out in the open
Last to go still standing until the clock stops
In the there is no present only pre history
All the caring fires smothered in love ashes

# Found Chaos

Second chance at everything
There is only the first time once
Turn around look back live
By then the past is out of sight
Fading from thought to nothing

Endless sea destiny to reach shore
Foot imprint rinsed by wave flat smooth
Dune sand between toes soft gritty
Survive to quest life dreamscape
Gone searching for aurora borealis

Universal opposites not attractive
Closed open blank a mind all noes
Caged in body isolated in space
Wondering what that last idea is
Wandering nomad sightless unknowing

Linden shadows move across floor fabric
Accented orange glow dusk zero degree
Then the moment of no light
Volcanic ash solar eclipse blind
Waiting for what that is there already

Helpless in wake of super nova immersion
What is known all erased illusion
Can not comprehend cosmos vastness
Entangled within a brain morass
Realize self knowledge then oblivion

*Ever good man is free.*
*Philo Judaeus 40 AD*

# Past Mist

Cascade vision scarlet hair lip smile face
Know love there walk thru dream place
Was a time we watched the fiery sunrise
Ended ashes in spirit forever gone prize

Only happy moment could do now feel
Everything we felt appears too surreal
Fun is all the what we really only had
Not to have those secrets would be sad

Moist lightless mist when lovers embrace
Once then hope for happiness now erase
In the finite oceans consumed by fervor
Those memories alive too will last forever

There was a special meadow no people go to
Mosquitoes lancing while in grass felt by toe
Making plans together ever holding hands
As our souls blew away like the arid sands

How could have lost that so long ago
Want still have is left for me to know
Imagine tress now love of distant past
We will never meet again...the die cast

# Passion Known

Emerged dripping slime from abyss
A mere occasion searching for bliss
Minds grip is only what we can hold
Reaching with gut seeking to be bold

Space between two minds is constant
Yet the heart throb can be distant
It is time when lips should be touching
Alas not the passion of bodies scorching

Can not go to the life past
Realizing nothing will last
No matter how fast we run
All we have is the now fun

A vision to walk again together
Not listing just be with each other
Never for a second the feeling alone
Yes knowing true love when gone

Silence following loss realization
Can never be undone live in illusion
Memories are captured like a fish
The featured savory marquee dish

# Stretch To What

Any the friend must be first met
Smile is as too for a memory kept
Every thing is beyond most a reach
Seek out the mind feelings to search

Traveling going through with self
Create masked scene cope with life
Run fast are still in place you were
One must take a challenge sincere

Faced the tempest with placid face
Can not forget a that last lost race
Think what live moment into future
Thought sent me turn mind torture

Memories of two bodies felt by both
Impossible away souls bond betroth
Melted in the thrall love a sincerity
Real happening felt tingle no fantasy

Lip touch piece of two hearts felt together
Time only goes away remembered forever
Personal deference may lead to confusion
Actual illusion sees reality pursue passion

# Horizon Reality

life not a drill rehearsal now
aware existence from inside out
when there is no wind for sail
do the thing that you can do
no word to indicate weak cause

to forget rule may be lethal
taught education may be remembered
involve specifics better learned
obvious reality illusion to delusion
passion more important than knowledge

love is fruit to climb tree for
find contentment in self first
useless to search elsewhere moot
caring is higher than justice
fix what needs when

try that which must be
moment it can be done
complete it the best way
focus right every time task
cloudy does not mean no sunshine

apocalypse is sure thing
can not prepare when ever
there is no advance plan
it is coming not stopping
instant tsunami rising on horizon

# Translucency

Life has so many transparent iron bars
When hit they shatter like canning jars
Seek forever something to keep in heart
The deeper one digs further away apart

Unknowing that which questionary
Embrace the flip side a visionary
Idea catalyst to energize soul bit
Need to dare fate destiny is in it

Want to grasp a why the reason
Birth life final wow such treason
Can not escape the one inevitable
End sentient road non laughable

Reality the present now happening
Wanting hugs to hold with loving
At this time think dikes are breachable
Past future moments away unreachable

Many miles away time that last kiss
Mind din floats deeper into the abyss
Searching into darkness between stars
Find hold a some one who really cares

# Sapien 410

Awareness subliminal instinct the hunt
Ninth grade a fourth down had to punt
Living seconds minutes hours irrelevant
It is now time red nose dog the moment

Blizzard conditions persisted thru the night
Massive amounts blowing snow to new height
Dawn wind subsided we went north from house
Down hill dense chest vegetation bird to rouse

Positioned on hill top faced the wind to start
Turned into white out wall beat of the heart
Then suddenly Soffie's ears went up straight
Quail covey rose and four met their fate

Moved over rise into dead forest ravine
She flushed up a few hens just routine
Another mile harvested pheasant dinner
Pushed thru weeds BOOM up down another

Exhaustion suddenly becomes to me known
Warmth gone hunts over no more to roam
Memorable wind crystal flake on face quest
Reflected a signature survival of the fittest

*Know Thyself. Love thy neighbor.*
*Thales of Miletus 546 BC*

# Chapter IX
## Camaraderie

*Happiness is when what you think,
what you say, and what you do
are in harmony.*

Mahatma Gandhi

# The Game That Was Team

At work one day a friend down the hall asked me if I would like to join the team in a mixed softball league. We started practices a couple of weeks before playing games against other teams across the campus.

It was slow high arc pitch softball with ten players on the field and three of them women. An umpire was provided that was given a roaster by the team coach and paper work was handed in after each game to the league organizers. There were seven innings, extra if it was tied. The ball count was two strikes, if you fouled after that you were out and three balls to walk. The fields were grass chalked lines down the 1$^{st}$ and 3$^{rd}$ base lines. No spikes just sneakers, jeans and T-shirts but we played hard as a team and no game was a push over.

That first year we all had fun but did not win enough to make the championship game then looked forward to the next summer. The team members became better friends over the winter months and when it came time to play again we were a seasoned veteran team ready to win. The infield positions were taken by those who had played for years, I was in center field. We played twelve to fourteen games, had some close ones that could have gone either way. When the dust settled we found our squad in the championship game.

It was played on the corner across from the old tennis courts south of the football stadium which now stands a building of the UI Hospitals & Clinics. There were no bleachers only chairs brought. The bar Joe's Place was recording the game for posterity. The infield was all dirt and the weather was ideal for a ball game clear sky, hot and dusty. The sun was only a factor in the far right outfield because of tall trees on the hill to the West, no wind.

It was a hard fought high scoring game that had us all dirty from our sweat mixed with dry dirt dust we played on.

The game came down to the bottom of the seventh inning, two outs and we were behind 13 to 16, bases loaded and I was up to bat with a count of two strikes and two balls. If I fouled we would lose the game, walk and the score would be 14 to 16 with two outs. So in my mind I wanted to win it right then.

It was a perfect pitch, high arc, reverse spin as I watched the stitches it come into the plate. Concentrating to keep my eye on the ball and swung as hard as I could. I hit it in the middle and the sweet part of the bat. The ball came off the bat ping rose straight over the pitchers head kept raising over second base and then way over the center fielders head. There were no fences and when the ball hit the hard ground it bounced and kept on rolling. As I rounded second base the fielder was just picking up the ball. In mind thought sprint. He had a good arm and as I rounded third base the coach yelled for me to stop but I did not just put my legs in over drive toward home plate. At that moment when my foot hit the plate the ball came in wide, long and the catcher missed it completely and I was safe with a grand slam homerun to win the championship.

I will always remember that moment, that time and that Team.

# Chapter X
## Insignificant Factor

*All the special illusions which mankind has raved about in religion, poetry, morals or philosophy, serve the purpose of deceiving and blinding the oppressed.*
*Leon Trotsky*

# Occasion Never Known Before

It was then a day that had never existed before
Date eight seven eleven twelve to twelve no encore
Eyes open sun light sensed like luminescent heaven
Slipped feet to floor ears heard caws sound of raven
The pendulum clock on wall still a vacuum air lock
Must be fleet armada readying to do battle left dock

Single parchment wall paper released from its glue
A wavy one piece of designer coarse fabric to view
Lying lifeless face down blocks aisle to make bed
Curl scroll placid form lies on floor nothing said
Like a distant gong echo faintly felt by the heart
Maybe an omen that one had left did so depart

Curious quest walk ensued eventually room to room
Seeking any other further signs of a possible doom
Two separate wall picture frames far from each other
Found floor not hanging on their brad did discover
I began wondering what this happening is it real
Experiencing gargantuan loss enter in surreal

A glancing to the left then right is time to water pet
Palm leaves over night turned brown no need to wet
Dear plant had gone shriveled vacant drooping form
Far from years of its flourishing lush green the norm
Wondered why such a friend was thriving then gone
A void but still in memory alive once standing alone

There was a bright flash of light a pause and then
Largest thunder shaking house rattling glass din
It was another incident of what I could not fathom
Distorted conscious happenings in single a day prism
Missing my distant love wishing she were here to hold
Splashed reality when a call came her soul passed told

It now is finally up to me everything like it has always been
Ner again look in her eyes only angel etched grave stone seen
Soft kiss is not just a kiss smile gone not a smile forever more
Ship lost at sea of eternity infinity never to return to its moor
Love remembrance exists in the mind to the end my of time
Caught up in the inevitable abyssal descent of paradigm

# Ships Going Bye

There are oceans in my mind full feeling of emotions
Having those past memoirs of non existent destinations
Lovers kisses that soon pass distant far like hard clay
Wanting an embrace just once more has gone away
Thoughts fade as the seconds days turn into seasons
Perhaps a new beginning another time other reasons

So many precious moments forever lost none now
Have become only withered ebbing waves past bow
Try to think looking for love that was or was not
Never not there is no chance loose less sought
Forget beginning and it is gone racing to the past
Not so feelings like a fishing line ready to be cast

Living wanting existent into next day's future
Dreams to be pursued goals made to nurture
There is no map or a path to again find love
Searching reaching some lofty heights above
Seems to be visible then vanishes gone and why
Amour is so very elusive one false move it will fly

This the time a middle of the game never to restart
Flowing into a win direction jousting to be not apart
Laughter thought nary mere illusion of crass innuendo
Music in the air bearing bull orchestra in crescendo
Time to drop the reins and let the thoroughbred loose
To not bottle up potential holding back inertia in a noose

Move forward perhaps go backward the only is present
Thinking what was or might have been a telescopic distant
Run to embrace the that which there to feel rejection
Still blessed having inner unfettered sincere affection
Children become more precious as the end nears to nothing
Deep awareness that eventually the fat lady will sing

Façade is lifted like the electric garage door
On a mission every year to donate to the poor
All encompassing eye on an aim not a target
Sleep dream wake walk focus never to forget
Need a companionship to hold a kiss on the lips
Letting ones own happiness in to the sailing ships

# Last Second Dream Lost

Without a dream how do we survive aimless
Walking depression alley to end of timeless
Moving from an awake day hours to night
Just skeleton decaying in bomb site blight
Radiation the reason out of womb we came
Never was or will be any two ever the same

Have lived ticket punched for your show
Out of your shoot a flying trying to glow
To grasp those opportunities passing in air
Any a grip must be attempted without err
Some things best slow others necessary fast
Totality a love rolling grass sandwich tryst

Each feeling existence as experience happening
Present decision choice mind changes adapting
Gaining knowledge along the non stop time line
Esoterically seeking any relationship to a sublime
Where have was been all my life so trapped
Imprisoned in societal hypnotic ego wrapped

Do not miss what is going around and pause
Concentrate all senses on the milieu its cause
From your alpha thru emotions ending omega
All a life living on floating plates over magma
Leap to unconscious coma life support plug pulled
Crawling my filthy gutter pariah mind grueled

Breathing in time air space oxygenating thought
Molecules supporting electrical synapse brought
Realizing at a point singularly one by one gone
Rationalizing all of our illusion with others alone
Not most find the easy way out to dismiss delusion
Birth beginning self is only continuum conclusion

Lost in the totality of non existent eternity
Does not matter in the here final eccentricity
Expanse of being long hard short easy minimal
Man is conclusively equal to small large animal
There is no ultimate escape of which is a primal
At the last second of game moment before final

# Placidity Evolves to Reality

Placidity of pool above falls clear cascading over cliff
Sound of gravity echoes white froth as splash in the rift
Racing away out of sight to distant places into eternity
Rivers at some times exhibit an ethereal type of serenity
Water is pulled to the next cyclic destiny a vast ocean
Nature never stops maybe held up but still in motion

A life flows on feelings thrives on what is being done
Everything is never before ever again poof then gone
Only brief moment to sense inner outer depth of quality
Look deep into other eyes search to find the sincerity
Apparent surface smooth gives no clue what beneath
Immerse to explore below what above veiled in sheath

Passion comes evolves then time enters center of soul
Take away compassion existence ceases work of whole
Some but very few square pegs fit into the round holes
Choice to swim the dark deep or wallow in sandy shoals
Mans heart and mind interactions what an enigma
Then take all the calculations come up with a sigma

If we had bird like wings we could fly far far away
Person made of many travels not one place to stay
Like chasing a mirage illusion turning to delusion
Ride road straight may get you quicker destination
And following bended trails seeking own ambition
Either becomes muted when end is just a fascination

Lost in one thought you may not come back to reality
Instant disappears down track vanished immortality
When one begins to see truth of that which you feel
It with an essence of purity cannot avoid to conceal
Where practice turns to magic all dreams born a hex
Superstitions existing we are ignorant to what next

See tiptoeing pixie dancing on point of pin
Her swirling twisting focusing mind in din
Awareness of our consciousness until finality
There is never a chance comes back futility
Life is a calm before cancer of life takes over
Know the precious what you have not forever

# Those Lost Dreams

Person is what inside out out side in personal history
From parents conception birth alpha omega one story
Start in a fetal position back roll over stand foot print
Child development formative years learning be sentient
Journeys to no where every where you want to go and be
Viewing vistas panoramas even when blind one can see

Each step we take is can only be one which is our own
Experiencing events on calendar with many others alone
Our sculpting into a singular shape etching a oneness
Unique artist's media you invent to form completeness
Forced into ancestral care we all were first free born
Imperative confrontation of those who want us forlorn

Naked we come naked we go clothed in between for show
Not every one is book or school smart more what you know
Reach out for that which is what some say can not be done
Brain brawn competition put in the record memorandum
Life is but a landscape we traverse move to another place
Always has been the man quest to find the ideal one face

Working the heart for purpose need concentration
Wanting what dreams are made of that destination
The beat of the music rhythm mimicking felt strings
Memories a many of tangoing singing a joy it brings
Walking toward the music on a hot summers night
Noise in the park concert feelings welling up bright

Not to let a second escape without being full
Hard not yet know there are so many times dull
Have the fun while you can will not be here forever
Wait it will be to late like water running to the river
Run down the road and catch a ride to the dance
Rub elbows kick up the feet spin round do the prance

At the end of the race make sure nothing left
What a wasted part of lifting in that final heft
Not go for when had the chance lost opportunity
Ever haunts thoughts could have been profundity
End of passage reminds of unconverted point past
Game goes to the end yet the memories forever last

*It was but yesterday we met in a dream.*
*Kahlil Gibran*

# From First All Encompassing

When to stop refraining the question I know the answer
Crossing the bow in an ethereal haze like a tap dancer
Awake asleep no one really fathoms what is happening
Seek to be in tune fooling self into over compensating
Living one life learning what grows with in each day
Perceptions melt to ash ember cold heart turns to clay

That which is always sought an only be there until found
We bind our minds to an ideal reality which we are bound
Time intermits all meaning as intellect waning to nothing
Distinctive visions accompany journey an occasional sting
Wanted a smooth sailing when obviously become sentient
Blind opaque processes from the on set of quest to opulent

Strenuous knowing that cheap trick of eventual non being
With no other alternatives is it preferable clearly seeing
We last as long as the patent exists then you are obsolete
Hiding behind multiple coats of paint yet so incomplete
Oneness inside evolves moment to moment to become stale
Can not turn back the clocks just try to adapt and avail

A vast microcosm existence universe earth own persona
Most lost in façade preconceived pod ova prima donna
All encompassed as an embryo emerging to be human
Nurtured in cultural superstition guided by shaman
Naïve filial teachings are difficult to break out of mold
Language individual personality influenced by what told

Music dance art shapes who we are what we will do
Custom familiarity reinforces what grand pa knew
Clan loyalties to protect livelihood is an essential
Outsiders' legions tend to want take is a universal
Some people are roamers and must trek to far lands
Moving foraging in forest across coastal dune sands

Ancient to modern time line is eons of sapiens history
Words written are only fiction interpretation quandary
Everything will become meaningless in a hundred years
For our bodies change into vacant forms no living peers
Move on today finding enjoyment in what is left now
Try to cope with coming final inevitability some how

# Living in Illusion of Life

What we have had lost will never return it is forever gone
Holding loved one in your arms soft kiss of lips now alone
Hard to dwell inside having precious moments memories
Ink penned on paper can not tell the love in heart stories
Touch of bare flesh eyes looking into the soul of another
Then comes the last breath taken lay to rest dirt to cover

Life from birth is only as long as we know who we are
Some of us travel long searching for what near to far
Our journey is over before begun crawling walking run
Surviving day to day after night sleep and rise of the sun
The last time our lids will close is not to be remembered
When the time clock stops all of existence is surrendered

I do not believe in anything for all there is only fate
Moving thru moments creating oneness then facilitate
None other can be who you are what you make yourself
Educate earn PhD mine coal in cave sit idly on a shelf
Any a choice of to go out the door is only up to you
Agoraphobic claustrophobic are many seen very few

We all live in our tiny boxes different many time zones
Were conceived evolved nurtured skin brain egos bones
Learning to adapt to what comes down the Milky Way
Moon stars planets visible during night bright sun day
All man is dieing like cells in a research lab Petri dish
So similar to the gilled unattended aquarium fish

Humanity is using up resources polluting to toxic end
Populations increasing no worry continue to pretend
Soon money will dry up for inane space exploration
Food production loses pace with stomach starvation
The doom of species is beyond being turned around
It is too late Armageddon is in sight to which bound

We think we are smart however just so insignificant
Compassion gone greed words to express what meant
Libraries books entire what written will cease to exist
Fading into burst disintegration into cosmic mist
Allusion of reality is so self delusion our illusion
Will not matter which way we go to the conclusion

# Life Unalienability

There are things you want to remember but can not
Some wish to forget yet stuck in mind like a knot
We live thru our time most dreams do not come true
Age moves on in years diminishes with less future
Is a waste to rue the passes dropped hesitating lost
Special the happy moments a holiday nog toast

All of so called history written fiction of author
That which happens can never be understood proper
Even if you dissertated this thought already gone
Some certain things become relevant A Bomb done
Interpersonal relationships intricate too profound
Whether which who you are the same destination bound

There is so much difference between the haves have nots
Those born silver spoons in mouth high odds they be bigots
The king is schooled pampered peon taught to work the plow
Elite immune from law innocent penniless may go to gallow
With callused hands know where have been and their place
Sometimes breeding in dogs human depends on their face

Unnoticed when not looking by people maybe unrecognized
Alyssa the wee fairy of Cinderella her mum there digitized
Not all are loved when traveling thru life's' time space
We came into this existence environment in own place
Call the shots as sentient to who what where and when
You are the your person now and until next second then

It is not the head crown that makes a royal king
True prince fosters philanthropy for those to bring
To give of ones self to those less fortunate hopeless
They can not be described in an instant pointless
Affluent not cognoscente of the quality their seeing
Living is a delusional me state of uncouth being

Some witness their life they live in day to day
And embrace the past candle light for to stay
It is not light or dark that makes who we are
Rather the sight even when blind such to dare
Reach for that impossible it is not improbable
Live the life your choose it is always unalienable

# Dawn of a Smile

Allusive passion lost in mix matrix of amour
Lust conscious flees thru the open moving door
Such an aphrodisiac that blinds the prudent
When immersed endeavor one to complaisant
Arms reach hug trapped caught in the moment
Feel the soft lips on lips elicit libido to foment

Emotions felt vanish in shadow of enigma
Lost heart throb evolves into a self stigma
A light wind caresses leaves in high ecstasy
Soaring in the pseudo depths of true fantasy
Walking thru the sun light of darkness bright
Reality dimension results in humanity blight

Spin the vane any direction still mind choice
The eyeless deaf dumb viewpoint without voice
There are not any two trails to what be truth
Path of true love comes but once being couth
When then found the diamond in grass rough
Should be happy joyous spend occasion to laugh

Ones compassion is transparent to those receiving
Words too maybe false but the heart undeceiving
Crawling then into a cave get to the sleeping bed
Every day travelings happenings all has been said
Feelings broken just holding on bashed to knees
Have always stood my ground never forced please

Want to show my inner self and must rise up over
Driven face down many times ascent into clover
Thinking ever so what that which befalls romance
Befuddlement of soul seeks one for that last dance
Can only see such hope of a vision will appear soon
Next post larva stage end will be eternal silk cocoon

My heart so longs for the vanished sweet love
Kept inside for so many years nothing above
So gone but that what want know to not come
Look round invisible site ere eyes only in poem
Last touching felt with those in past part of me
Oh alas resigned to rest in my fate that it to be

*True love is rooted in the recognition of the moral
and mental qualities of the beloved.
Baron Richard Von Krafft-Ebing*

# Moment Past

Some times a fear raises its scaled head
Smooth skin viper hollow fangs to dread
Flinch an instant injection blood stream
Then perchance enter into a fatal dream

What is the real me face never to flee
Did not know life's eventual totality
Slept thru one third of my now existence
Hence remember repressed wish presence

True love does not come and go forever it stays
Even though the others have gone in many ways
Slumber maybe dwell in twilight snooze zone
Some have heart another pseudo monotone

My only ball room dance was born of honor
Exiled compassion king never rein over poor
It sounds like my happy music resounding
Escape from tyranny profundity pounding

Retract to inner cell prison can not touch
Forever be who am none can feel reproach
Not all have been brought up being truly kind
Others find it by the familial ties that bind

Weather unchangeable whether one wants
Time of flood that never was before daunts
It is now it is this day to say the good-by
Some never say 'I love you' don't even try

Work hard at one level transcend to another
Canst speak how people feel not even brother
Being from the cold north she the deep south
Had to communicate with a different mouth

Is compassion set in your private dynasty
Who can be saved from their own destiny
Caught between ground and the air
Works of great fine art is for to share

What appears to be fact may be science fiction
Smiles shines in those eyes that see perfection
We create false monoliths to greats of the past
Yet need to take a moment to bait and cast

To see others hurting not my hand
Some have made sadism their fatherland
We course through our short lives seeking
Have choice to do our best while protecting

Life without any reason is despot season
Festering like a cancerous malady lesion
Truth is an elusive enigma in the mind
Many quest their entire life never to find

Search the wisdom of our forbearers
Have pity on those who became torturers
Venture a promise alms to unfortunate
Less than more to those living in hate

Night light be day in winter hemisphere moon
Friendship loyalty are far above hot air balloon
You go to books to find the answers that are not there
Meditate to reach soul but its over should still care

Living in an uncivilized world is the great demise
How people talk and act seems not at best very wise
Only way I am able to grasp understand being
Has been a life time of not knowing just seeing

When gone change will continue to happen by moment
At least the consolation will no longer be my torment
Earth humanity is but everything and so to nothing
Explored for compassion found evil never stop giving

# Yesterday Not Tomorrow

...and feelings felt begin to knock knock to be heard
Façade crack shell open fell away escape flies a bird
Soar to heights unknown a new life form what it is
Purpose says direction what destination mind quiz
Questions arise into mind thought where have I been
Is there a real existence or what does anything mean

Everything gone before past lost missed
Wish she were here for her lips to be kissed
Own to do best what is within my only deep
Know nothing neither possible what can keep
Do not reach ever extend to a place to mope
Attempt not what you want is no way hope

What the charades we played in memory caves
Children in adult skins stories taken to graves
Every scheduled event now only illusionary fun
Danced gym floor bands we knew fantasy begun
Some few stayed together others no adhesive glue
Wanted dreams to come true but vanished flew

True friends find each other in any season
A caterpillar pupates course of ontogeny reason
If wanted it did not appear no consequence
Never was an iconic benevolent equivalence
Lost faith in others when they were not into me
Live all life moments that may seem to naught be

Make no way for tomorrow today is at hand
We all live the now existing on own little island
Challenges to take next breath will not last forever
Try what you can when you can for goal to endeavour
Where are you from yesterday but tomorrow
We want a bit of happy times to not borrow

# Has Been Went

Where have I been all my life
Wasting away time on things of trite
Missing the boat dealing with others strife
Hesitation too much on what is not just right
Can not ever go back into history start again
Plan with past learned knowledge quest to attain

Make the most of what your have now
There may not be another chance to aspire
Set the goal so when reached you may bow
Place yourself in experiences to study acquire
Become master of your own existent psyche
Hope to reach some happiness you can see

Get up after sleepless night out door a raining
What to do today in house readings writing
Look past theorize forward mind in training
Research anthropology stone age painting
Search deep within what really matters
Before swim dip toe cool or warm waters

It is here that I know not why alive
Reason existence philosopher expound words
Approach understand fact is name survive
Mortal destiny skips no sapien peon lords
All come that exact moment when conscious
Realization may cause some to become nauseous

Open eyes melancholy permeates muscles want to stay in bed
A sense it is only my hollowed sadness just sing the blues
Nothing to get up for day free to have more sleep instead
Dejection of what was a gone sombers emotion leads to rues
Damp cold fog in your awakeness when be the doom
Lost track have become another person to loom

Been many years endured swallowed all of the bitter
Yield to life's forces to see and grasp understand
Never would she want me to end up another quitter
Get back in the race begin again sing in a band
Music follows us always what heard humming your song
Reach for sweetness continue to progress as you go along

# Labyrinth

Drew the line in the sand for my own self mind set life
Lip service ignored pupils fixed dilated no more strife
No on retires unless gone except in their small mind
Each finds a niche in a nook of a model of his kind
Stock car comes into the pits fuels tires out into race
Be who you are what you can need not change face

Uneven is everywhere on curved globe around the bend
Level is but an illusion on a gauge just a measured trend
Skewed learning and experiencing try to guess what next
At some point one makes a decision or not in silent vortex
Reach out for the other side of syntax what is before death
Will never know what is going to happen not even last breath

Tread bottom boots imprinting mark artefact in sand not odd
Triceratops mastodon foot placement leave traces as they plod
Change the keys in music solo is to slip paddle behind back
To the other side of canoe stern a voice aria in a mind tract
Hide falsity inside a truth eventually emerges non efficacious
Egregiousness unattended increases exponentially into crisis

I want to love deeply for another to be held close
Laugh talk dance walk hold hands embrace Eros
Have a relationship of mutual respect honor adoration
Something substantial lasting to the final destination
The river of lasting romance flows chasing destiny quest
Wanting to reach a happiness nothing less than the best

*True love is rooted in the recognition of the moral*
*and mental qualities of the beloved.*
*Baron Richard Von Krafft-Ebing*

# By My Side As One

You do not have to pretend a real friend lasts a life time
A beside partner always an ally and helpfully sublime
Wanting to be together sharing special moments daily
Walking through the rain playing in first snowfall gaily
Being there as a brother or sister when one is needed
Never rude or confrontational only nice never conceited

You are blessed when a person is with you thick and thin
Regardless what the score may be big loss or barely win
Sometimes it is one in a billion or maybe never will be
Heart is a lonely hunter doomed forever into eternity
There are pseudo people with masks to hide insincerity
Showing in their voices and actions obvious temerity

You can run round the world in search of non stop
Climb highest mountain and embed a flag at the top
Try to be noticed by anyone yet you become invisible
Realizing in the end what sought is just impossible
It is vividly clear giving up is a waste of what is left
Begin again again to live short journey sanity kept

Must hitch a seat on the fantasy roller coaster ride
Swim the lakes and oceans to get to the other side
Then to find nothing that has not been found before
Keep plodding thru the blizzard blindly wanting more
Going around the corner many times to see what is there
Need to have some purpose to like for you are somewhere

As an alone man who looks in the mirror to find face
Peers deep into own eyes trying to understand his place
Insignificant in a vast of space destiny up to individual
These are no straight lines round earth numbers not equal
What seen not instantaneous thru tissue liquid into brain
A longer route of travel sentiently after having read quatrain


The bottom line is not the end because there is still the beyond
Longer it takes to forge a friend the more it becomes profound
There is always some hope even in an advanced age to the last
Continue putting bait on the hook swing pole back then cast
Fishing for what might be alive under the placid surface
Finality cannot be in my vernacular is ever to stay in chase

# We Live From Our Past

There are things you want to remember but can not
Some wish to forget yet stuck in mind like a knot
We live thru our time most dreams do not come true
Age moves on in years diminishes with less future
Waste to rue all the passes dropped hesitation lost
Special the happy moments a holiday window frost

All of that written history pure fiction of the author
Event which happens can never be understood proper
Even if one to dissertate this thought already is gone
A certain thing becomes relevant like an A Bomb done
Interpersonal relationships so intricate way too profound
Whether which who you are the same destination bound

Is too much difference between the haves and have nots
Those born silver spoons in mouth high odds they be bigots
A king is schooled pampered peon taught to work the plow
Elite immune from law innocent penniless may go to gallow
With callused hands know where have been and their place
Often times breeding in dogs humans depend only on face

Noticed when not looking by some maybe unrecognized
Dear fairy Alyssa of Cinderella her picture was digitized
Not all loved to fullest when going thru lifetime space
Came into this existence environment left own trace
Call the shots use a sentient to who what where when
You are the your person now and next second then

A soul has its intrinsic resonance in echo canyon
Voice aria just foot print in a disappearing union
Friends are those who listen with their heart sincerely
Come to understand that not all of what felt is reality
Learn what can adapt to extenuating circumstance
Hope needs our energy in order that we may enhance

People are better than no people they keep you going
Real hard job defeat is not an option continue doing
Extraordinarily we exist one singular from first fathers
Door opens signifies end and beginning smiles with others
We are all wired different no control even over self heart
End of life realize youth choice consequential then depart

# Idyllic Muse

Dreaming floating like feather thru opening in sky
Pastel hues of aurora borealis like vortex to mystify
Alit soft in idyllic garden flowers land of Xanadu
Kaleidoscopic haze engulfs body of fermata in situ
Magical music mesmerizes meaning of the heart
Shrill melodic singing lyric that will not depart

Thrill to hear real passion expressed by syrinx tune
Feel alive as sun crossed gaze evolves to stars moon
My world is a stage to release what thrives inside
Embrace that which deepest there nothing to hide
Yearning a role that defines inspirational dream
Ache for the one single moment you can scream

Live be immortal great death is not end of life
Rather what dies within while living in strife
Gift is a fantasy of illusion to be who you are
Be alive each day to conquer fears to go far
Mortality lasting but just a lightenings flash
Forever remember time to time then end dash

Self create your art piece in the arena of theater
Bond with those others naught anything greater
If I only could whisper louder so maybe to hear
Must release that beast burst forth with no fear
Give to the audience all to take it is right now
Back down not an option no pressure just pow

Suddenly the strange majic never ever other
Make most of all days have one then another
Something has a firm grip on my voice tight
Walk talk thought consumed mind just right
Dont act like those others must be a whole you
Have a little more sometimes less then be true

Grasp what is in hand before gone moving on
Sing solo soul thought an ad lib tis your song
Can not be born again dont turn away to fly
Destiny is in ken of autumn rain a time to try
As the world starts again each moment of day
There is only one thing for sure that is to bay

*Everything great is just as difficult to realize*
*as it is rare to find.*
*Baruch Spinoza*

# ChapterXI
## Daring to Live Love

*Conquer yourself rather than the world.*
*Rene Descartes*

# Greatest Dive

Learned how to swim when four at five competitively in Hasting, NE. At that time began to go off the three meter diving board eventually diving. The family moved to Cedar Rapids, IA. Every summer for many years we went on a two week vacation mainly for my father to fish in the lakes and streams of MO KS OK CO WY MT NE S & N DK MN and Canada.

During those times swam lakes with my younger brothers oaring a hand built ten foot wooden row boat beside me no life preservers. Also did some Scuba diving. When there were cliffs would dive. At home would dive from the three meter hundred times a day doing swans, twists, backs, inwards, gainers and multiple summersaults. One summer won a diving trophy at Elmcrest Country Club City Swimming Meet.

In 1964 when CR Washington High School won the state swimming championship at the University of Iowa Field House Pool guys went jumping off the ten meter platform. Climbed the wooden latter and dove into eleven feet of water twice, what a thrill, so high, straight down, no fear.

Was drafted into the US Army and deployed to Germany. One day went to the Mannheim Swimming Pool a magnificent facility maybe two football fields in size where hundreds of people were swimming, sunning, walking around. It had lots of grass, Olympic size pool with a warm up area, fifty meter straight swimming, ten lanes, one and three meter spring boards and five and ten meter platforms into seventeen meters of water. Swam around for a while and noticed a line for the one meter board just kids. Why not dive? Went to the three meter and did a couple of one and a half dives my favorite. What the heck began to scale the latter to the ten meter platform. When reached the flat top what a view it was to look out over the berg. Then noticed all the people had stopped doing anything and were looking high up to a lone diver.

Gazed at the distant faces for a short moment then curled my toes over the metal ell edge, stood erect, arms at my side, slowly raised them to shoulder level hands stiff, head up, leaned forward, pushed off out and up in a perfect flying swan dive straight to the bottom. When pierced the surface I heard applause.

A month later by best friend Mark from Malibu, CA and I took an eight day leave from Frankfurt thru Zurich, Switzerland to the Spanish Isle of Mallorca capital Palma. It was sun sun sun clouds only on the horizon. Had an opportunity to fly to Algiers for a one day tour by an attractive French/Algerian guide that we stereotypically GI's flirted with and she did not mine the attention.

When landed and exited the plane there were military soldiers every twenty feet, both sides with M-16 rifles and sun glasses. Our passports were confiscated at the terminal desk and they told us to stay with the tour. We traveled by bus to a café and ate local food then walked thru the Casbah and the main street. We did escape with passport and life to fly back to Palma.

The next day we met up with two Swedish women on vacation in our hotel cantina. I was drinking ten cent bottles of local champagne and looked around to see two beautiful eyes staring at me and moved over to her table and she invited me to sit down. Men stayed in the men hotel and women stayed at the women hotel, strict no visitation up to the rooms, guards were on duty.

Her name was Ulla of Sollentuna, Sweden. We spent the night up from the beach in a clearing in the bushes, on a blanket, rapped in each others arms all night. When the dawn came we got dressed and walked to our hotels for showers reliving the night in my mind a hundred times. Mark had hooked up with her friend Britt and the four of us rented a car and drove to home of Robert Graves, Past Poet Laureate of England. We had been reading his poetry.

"Every vote cast is cast away

Every choice is the wrong choice

For how can truth hover between alternatives?" Found the villa and knocked on the fortified gate door for a long time, nothing and then went down to Cala Deya, consisting of a cantina and many shacks and some boats on racks. The sand beach was facing west out to the Mediterranean Sea with cliffs on both sides. We sat in chairs with others drinking wine, sunning our bodies and enjoying the ambience of being in an idyllic setting. A couple of fishing boats came into the bay and paused at the base of the right butte, the boys climbed up to a spot about five meters high on the right side. After several jumps they got into their boats and came to shore.

The local wine was in our blood and I said to Mark, "...if you take a picture I will dive off the top of the cliff". He being from Malibu the dare capital of America said he would catch me in mid air. I stripped to my Speedo kissed Ulla and dove into the surf to swim the two hundred yards to the base of the cliff. There was a path: up thru the brush and the rocks were well worn and hot from the sun. About half way up the path ended and the rocks were rougher. It took me about thirty minutes to get to the top. When reaching the summit what a view of the bay and sea. Looked to the beach and saw the small humans gathering to watch. Close to a hundred had come out of the cantina, shacks, the fishermen and my friends. I waved to them moved forward to curl my toes over the sharp edge of the precipice and looked down. I stood there for a minute or two looking at the people, out to sea and then to the water below. I could not see the surface it was as clear as glass all the way to the bottom and knew it was at least fifty feet deep from a previous swim over the spot.

Concentrating that my body would have to be exactly perpendicular, making fists with my hands, holding them tight together to make a hole for my head to go thru the surface. After all of the preliminaries I stood erect arms at my side no fear. With my chin up lifted my arms shoulder high leaned forward and pushed hard into the air like a bird.

I slowly rotated focused on hitting the surface true. My flying swan position toes pointed slowly moved arms over my head ducked my head and hit the water perfect. Must have gone twenty-five feet down, turned around to swim up with millions of champagne-like bubbles. Burst into the air, waved to the shore and swam. Walking out of the surf Ulla hugged me real tight and said, "I thought you were going to die".

Mark did take the photo when in mid flight and said people applauded when I waved after coming up.

When we got back to base I read in the paper a GI dived off a cliff on the Spanish mainland hit some rocks and died.

A few months later I drove forty hours straight thru Denmark, and riding on two ferries to Sollentuna and spent two wonderful weeks with Ulla her friends and family, mother plus five brothers and sisters with children.

# tempting fate

tuesday drove north to the rivers placid lake
wanting that experience of a oneness with nature
in open air wind cloudy sky weather water exercise
thirteen foot aluminum canoe colored green black brown
strapped atop my mode of transportation on wheels turning

normal January spitting snow flakes
strong northerly zero cold heavy overcast
causing two feet high white caps spreading alee
to quarried rocks checking soil erosion east of bridge

gathered placed heavy stone most forward as ballast
push off perpendicular into cresting crashing splashing waves
last instant hopped into metal seat began trip for hours
the ever constant paddling warms the blood brain
no sweat perpetually in motion heat to the body
eddies swirl aft dissipating into nothingness

traveling a natural pre historic pathway
passion stimulating thought imagination creativity
blown hair twisting perceived essence of alive here now
leg arm shoulder exert power propelling pushing posterior
momentum surging only mere inches at per each stroke
cutting bow prow directed straight into wanted direction
rolling motion over the waves occasional spray in the air
moisture accumulation dripping across face off the chin
blinking eyes focus on course to unknown destinations

paused on a beach in a cove sheltered from the gale
found a beautiful flinted chalcedony projectile point
anthropological omen unliving alive in spirit this day
no other boats no people on the shore no houses in view
two flying high crows battling elements wings flapping


positioned to go down wind return to the starting site riprap
surfing on the icy waves atop the world at times felt weightlessness
feathering craft rocking side to side dipping in swales peaking up
past experience kept speed balance in a right spot of frothing curls


brazen to tempt fate in a primal dare of survival
capsizing would have been a defiant end of any life
emotion of exhilaration defined who I am to myself
ultimate pleasure so testing inner being to the limits
action fun happiness wow and endorphin high five


never always alone surrealistically ethereal
diving free falling to an abyssal depth of feelings
totally immersed in a quick sand moment presence
cerebral cortex strumming mandolin chords of by soul

# Delirium

entered unconsciousness by concussion
drip drip dripping of my blood
crushing of broken bones
massive internal bleedings
time stops never

awareness of awakenings
barely called help none came
slept all day for weeks
forever experience in brain fog

lost parts of memory
cognition substantially diminished
people skills are totally gone
not fit for human consumption

surging to regain self image
cmas at home no one else
80 percent blind
aloneness all encompassing

phlebotomies IV's meds
CAT Scan 1st surgery
lungs are breathing
alive now illusion
time will stop

# From There To Nowhere

Traveled a distance to the window to see life
The drapes were closed and no living was seen
Opened the curtains it revealed a cement wall
Eyes created frustration nothing was revealed

Went to the door to reach to the other side
The gate was locked and there was no key
A feeling spreads across the mind all is lost
Just to sit down cease trying is to give up

Knocked on the door it opened into darkness
Unexplained non entity a void unexplainable
If or when I wake will I know what is reality
Swimming up the waterfall delusion illusions

Have gone from not knowing to knowing not of
What must be on the other side can not be there
For it could not exist without evidence in sight
Not seeing when there is nothing to see it not

Fantasy comes to the forefront when is unplain
Nonexistent reality fails the litmus test of gone
Followed by the most confusion that a life has
What never brought needs to be pursued to get

Falling in to a love over and over is not love
A tripping over best things that ever happened
Misses hitting the target longed for many times
Can never make it to that wanted happy ending

Crying toxic tears inflicting cancer to the floor
Ran away as fast as the tortoise sleep walking
To remember what can not be forgotten future
Wheeling up the upgrade to the swamp water

Refusing to understand what is an unobvious
Spinning in a whirl pool the dizzied lost heart
Feelings stuck in the vast crevasse unyielding
Snagged by the barbed wire trapping the felt

Surrounded by a starless infinite space vacuum
Sucked inward osmosis the other side outward
A metamorphic pre ending of the hatched ovum
Swallowed by the decomposition of a putrid rot

Flying away to the never there ever not
Sounds similar to an nonemergence plot
Then ending what went in then out caught
An insect landing on glue is too slow gone

Existential lost remnants of life fate
The grand slam bridge cards dealt made
After the game play out the door depart
Found not what seeking unrequited love

# Morel Thought

early morning calm
din of drip dripping of dew
cascade slashing life to forest factories

plethora cover shades of green brown yellow
patches of mayberry velvet moss fungi fern flora
big surface machine blanket heterogeneous floor

small serengeti grazers carnivores
anthropoid nematode arachnid grasses
rodent aviary fodder pupas larvae hidden
natural selection must camouflage survival

humid warm light brief shower
then burst of sun nuclear radiation
slowly trekking over surface topography
spatial rotational a planet on axis space
active photosynthesis plant result animal life

distant caw colony crow
song of lone finch in bush
robin cardinal symphonies
faint trickle waterfall gravity
eroding sandstone to sands of time

smell that organic earthy decay
on the light breeze lilac sweetness
driving insects pollen sensorial myriad
breathe olfactory stimuli strong scent
constantly elicit taste in salivary liquid
secretions fill brain referencing memory

slow and measured step bending torso
search ground for ultimate hunt query
an amble roving over rolling hill rill
meadow briar ravine fallen elm oak
branches leaves nettle bacterial life

alone never not alone there
foliage rustle stand erect turn round
duel eye to eye deer herd in frozen motion…
an instant returning to trail tranquil gone
experience serene peaceful co existence
predator prey not this day tomorrow

epiphany to feel surface of plucked morel
journeys quest successful primordial need
following culinary ingestion to nurture sapien

# Just Mine to Stay Alive

Living from the suns brightness some less night moon shine
Take away the light into a blindness mind adapts in kind
Stamp out that distant solar energy nothing would survive
The only instinctual thing from birth is to thrive to stay alive
Not one can save that singular person you have become inside
Naturally primordially a coming to us ebbing with the tide

To pray is for the prayer more a catharsis for the living
When the dieing have become the dead it is the ending
When we look down from a surgeon's eye to preserve a life
It be just an instant in the time of the mankinds strife
Initiate all the means and promote to continue a breath
Yet in wars efforts are made to maximize the enemy death

No any stories are like yours you are the only regal
Singing for oneself thru a heart and mind is integral
Aesthetic feelings flow to the central core of my being
Fountain spurting to reality consciousness emanating
Flowing down mountain sides like lavas destinations
Seeking more constantly of passion in the inspirations

Who are we pseudo alpha omega of family tradition
Just to embrace what one has in the heart satisfaction
Nothing permanent holds what you can be to the final you
My journey is not a destination when it's time now the cue
Being a questful mind what done did is over flow passionate
Keeping a one focus on what ever is important to initiate

Staying alive varies with who what where one is to live
Harder to the wants dreams needs and to survive
A constant swing from goals ambitions failures success
Our one ever changing moments exist as a human process
Situation most times unplanned lead us to the unexpected
Adapting or dismissing change a part of the road neglected

Justifying anything is up to the individual choice
Singing classical opera superior depends on voice
Competing in Olympic decathlon is for some their lot
So many struggle slides down rope to hold to the knot
Survival is not an option to anyone ever on this earth
Best we can do is stock in wood keep warm from hearth

# Love Never Leaves Heart

Where did your love go from yesterday
our lips met we said good-by
you did not come back
we were going to be together forever
live happily ever after
like in a fairy tale

Drove to the cemetery
winged angel etched on stone
you are in my heart until it beats no more
smile is a portrait in my cerebrum gallery
walk where we use to still there beside

Feelings now are not of grief fate acceptance
fantastic moments shared to treasure when thought
a life journey then rest in the mind
joy in what was held embraced hugged
remember a day a time for no other reason
soaring over illusionary rainbows

Winters would be cold but the memories

*Our greatest glory consists not in never falling,*
*but in rising every time we fell.*
*Oliver Goldsmith*

# Bang

There once was a time when
others life situation feelings
dragged on me began to descend then

SNAP

The mind imploded exploded
into a trillion pieces
never to be the same
ever again

Almost slipped into the pit further
grasped hope and held on
to survive another day

Have to exist with the agony
loss of dignity impaired cognition
What did happen at this
moment in by life

Can not walk in the past
each second is another second gone
Repair prepare for tomorrow live now
Start over open the brain to be receptive
Work to learn try to find who I am

Why are we here only to leave
when the ship sails away
on the final voyage

This is the one question that has
all conscious beings trying to answer
without success rationally

# Today is Now

There is an ocean in my mind full of emotions
Giving those past memories non existing destinations
Thought fades as the second then day turns to seasons
Perhaps a new beginning another time other reasons
Lover kiss soon will pass distant afar like minute in clay
Try to reach embrace hope that it will never go away

So many a precious moment lost gone none now
Have become only those lost thoughts in me some how
Try to think looking for love that was or was not
Never ever again there is no chance unless sought
Forget the last end it is gone racing to the past
Not so feeling life a fishing line ready to be cast

Living wanting existent then next day future
Dreams to pursued goal made to nurture
There is no map or path to again find love
Searching to reach lofty heights up above
Seems to be visible then vanishes gone why
Love is very elusive slight move it will fly

This is the time of the middle game not to restart
Must flow into main direction jousting to be not apart
A future will never be what you plan it to be just so
Singing in the shower hearing orchestra in crescendo
Time to drop the reins and let the thorough bred loose
Not bottle up potential holding back inertia in a noose

Move forward can not go backward the only is present
Thinking what was or might have been a telescope distant
Run to embrace the air that is there to feel rejection
Blessed to have unfettered deep sincere love and affection
Children become more precious as the end nears to nothing
Deep awareness that eventually the fat lady will sing

Façade is lifted like the electric garage door
On a mission every year to donate to the poor
All arms encompassing an aim not a target
Sleep dreams wake walk focus never to forget
Need a companionship to hold love kiss on lips
Never not letting loose happy the necessary quips

# Final Analysis

All of those human beings I have loved and lost
A part of me went with them some at high cost
Life goes non stop continues on to the final end
What has happened experienced some dividend
An instant of epiphany when you did your best
All in the past becomes important in your quest

That moment when a zygote happens we are alive
Nurtured in youth by others become person to thrive
Consumption of sustenance knowledge daily existence
Travels an individual journey always in ones presence
Learning what takes us into sadness perchance happiness
Mistakes become known promotes cognitive consciousness

Living too much in our memories takes away our now
A flash becomes but a photograph of a marriage vow
The past moment is most present just ever always there
Future nebulous predictions said some could beware
Swimming laps over again forges your physicality bound
Totality of health mind body enlightenment to be sound

Occasionally boat lists in the tempest of thought
Sometimes feel as falling from trapeze then caught
Insignificant bug spider web consumed turned to dust
Engine increases speed to destination like epee thrust
Strike to the inner heart of issue certainly forthright
Searching and reaching for that one idea so bright

In the autumn when leaves coloring think this the end
Snow flakes in space to ground shovelling back to bend
Amidst the dormant winter skiing much delight
Yet thoughts entering thoughts so many contrite
It takes the warming in spring to thaw the braw
Authors pencil to compose artists char coal to draw

Finality realization that life's purpose amazing
Wheels turning mind horizon feelings tantalizing
Be what feel maybe mediocrity still who you are
Acid helixes evolving complex tactile syntax fare
We product vanity humility protect things loved
Survive in family then make statement be proved

A crisis in mans psyche only a self anomaly
Earthquake tsunami forces non premonitory
Listen with no ears feelings vibrations ethereal
These silent notions may be cause of your survival
There is no panacea of the future only a happening
Fading with the sunlight of an aged cornea imaging

# Chapter XII
## Epilogue

*There is nothing which can better deserve our patronage than*
*the promotion of science and literature. Knowledge is in every*
*country the surest basis of happiness.*
*George Washington – Address to Congress 8 Jan 1790*

# We Were Washington
## MCMDXVI

Academics activities achievements athletics arts and applause
Preparing Senior student for future work college life ever after
Six hundred months removed crossing millennium line now
Reunion of class to see old friends to celebrate being alive still
It was our glory year not forgotten ever in heart as the best

Entered naïve Sophie denizens graduated Senior royalty
Lockers by homerooms stairs elbow to elbow granite floor
Admiral Fitzsimmons a well respected helmsman for success
Teachers an ego menagerie left tight up down middle gone
Came from Franklin McKinley to mix into the best ever us

Victory Bell rung Monday mornings in honor of Warrior Wins
Ontogeny tends to recapitulate phylogeny Iola Tillapaugh
Tennis thork baseball crack football punt French Horn sounds
Seaquins synchronicity placid surface like Ballet Orchestra
Albino reptile fang entered teacher ambulance hospital fine

Hear of the midnight ride of Paul Revere charging up the hill
Staked out a claim ten by ten spread a little bit of magic dust
Miracle then happened on that grassy slope appearing a big **66**
One fifty-five Hwy 13 '56 Red Corvette Honor Society Pin Golf par
Homecoming festivities Queen crowned Democracy in Forum

Pre holiday events concerts vacation then it became our year
Exchange students Columbia Thailand France Surveyor Debate
Art class posing drawing paint sculpture history of greats awe
Epiphany moment puberty MUDACO Government Girls Boys State
Hall smell baking class bread cafeteria aroma pool chlorine

Game Kingston lights cheerleaders Pom Pom performing legs
Warm up passes footballs goal posts players relatives dates
Big band marching playing into night air aura ambience
Pep Club Letterman's Club student body cheering section
Pre game concession post game concussions unrealized

Intramural ping pong archery bowling gymnastics Life Saving
Thespians all the singing voices and those who remain silent
Tweaking carburetor dropping tran smoothing wood to stain
Languages English Spanish German Latin French Russian
Swimming with mentally retarded YWCA St Luke's Candy Striper

'Walked on the Wild Side' just being a 'Curious Savage' and
Singing like 'The Music Man' 'The Adventurers' motorcycles
Telephone long distant operators with head sets on Scouting
Rifle range under water pool window weight room reps Algebra
State Basketball Championship game came up short we were there

Mr "A" missed…was the most compassionate person in my life
Birthday Ball with Martha and George Hospitality Club Sewing
FBLA mixer well attended there is more than books in library
Learn skills at MeToo Wagner Printing machine shop typing
'Fete des Rois' French only spoken in Paris idyllic venue

Wonder what it would have been like if girls had had sport
Girls Rec Assoc Future Nurses of America State Swim Champions
When you go thru Washington you become part of the legacy
In our final scene we graduated in the sanctum of the gym
It was purely the special year that was

*From Washington on graduation day we'll have to journey*
*on...memries of our high school days will live with in our hearts.*
*Alma Mater Washington – Richard DuBois*

*What we have once enjoyed*
*and deeply loved we can*
*never lose; for all that we loved*
*deeply becomes part of us.*
*Helen Keller*

*...wisdom, compassion and courage---*
*these are the three universally recognized*
*moral qualities of man.*
*Confucius*

...moment precious...

# Tire Swing Photograph

I bought the film, used my Minolta camera
to take the picture, hand developed the
negative in a roll canister, used an
enlarger to expose the print on photographic
paper, developed the print with the dip
method (developer, fix, water wash, dry),
mounted it on the poster board.

Ken Krizan

Printed in the United States
By Bookmasters